Divine Radiance in Human Evolution

DIVINE RADIANCE
IN HUMAN EVOLUTION

Diarmuid O'Murchu

ORBIS BOOKS
Maryknoll, New York 10545

Founded in 1970, Orbis Books endeavors to publish works that enlighten the mind, nourish the spirit, and challenge the conscience. The publishing arm of the Maryknoll Fathers and Brothers, Orbis seeks to explore the global dimensions of the Christian faith and mission, to invite dialogue with diverse cultures and religious traditions, and to serve the cause of reconciliation and peace. The books published reflect the views of their authors and do not represent the official position of the Maryknoll Society. To learn more about Maryknoll and Orbis Books, please visit our website at www.orbisbooks.com.

Copyright © 2025 by Diarmuid O'Murchu.

Published by Orbis Books, Box 302, Maryknoll, NY 10545-0302.

All rights reserved.

Scripture quotations, unless otherwise noted, are from New Revised Standard Version Bible: Catholic Edition, copyright © 1989, 1993 National Council of the Churches of Christ in the United States of America. Used by permission. All rights reserved worldwide.

No part of this publication may be reproduced or transmitted in any form or by any means, electronic or mechanical, including photocopying, recording, or any information storage or retrieval system, without prior permission in writing from the publisher.

Queries regarding rights and permissions should be addressed to: Orbis Books, P.O. Box 302, Maryknoll, NY 10545-0302.

Manufactured in the United States of America.

Manuscript editing and typesetting by Joan Weber Laflamme.

Library of Congress Cataloging-in-Publication Data

Names: O'Murchu, Diarmuid, author.
Title: Divine radiance in human evolution / Diarmuid O'Murchu.
Description: Maryknoll, NY : Orbis Books, [2025] | Includes bibliographical references and index. | Summary: "A Christian theology incorporating insights from paleoanthropology, evolutionary biology, and archaeology"— Provided by publisher.
Identifiers: LCCN 2024055242 (print) | LCCN 2024055243 (ebook) | ISBN 9781626986121 (trade paperback) | ISBN 9798888660676 (epub)
Subjects: LCSH: Theological anthropology—Christianity. | Evolutionary biology—Religious aspects Christianity. | Science and religion.
Classification: LCC BT701.3 .O53 2025 (print) | LCC BT701.3 (ebook) | DDC 233/.11—dc23/eng/20241206
LC record available at https://lccn.loc.gov/2024055242
LC ebook record available at https://lccn.loc.gov/2024055243

Contents

Introduction vii

1. **A Context Too Long Neglected** 1
   Theological Change in the Twenty-First Century / 2
   Our Bankrupt Anthropology / 5
   Classical Greek Anthropology / 8
   We Are the World / 10
   Individuality, Relationship, and Personhood / 13
   The End of Dogmatism / 15

2. **Our Human Story and Divine Revelation** 19
   Christian Salvation / 20
   Our Sacred Human Narrative / 22
   Entering Deep Time / 27
   The Human Narrative as a Faith Story / 28

3. **God's Chosen Earthlings** 33
   Earthlings at Home in Creation / 36
   Our Earthiness in Focus / 39
   Programmed to Cooperate / 41
   The Relational Matrix of Christianity / 44
   Reworking the Theological Tradition / 49

4. **The Grace of Human Creativity** 51
   The Patriarchal Context / 52
   Reclaiming Our Authentic Story / 54
   Our Ancient Artistic Flair / 55
   Imagination, Visualization, Discrimination / 57
   The Artistic Flair / 59

The Religious Dimension / 62
Where Grace Abounds / 65

5. **God beyond the Culture of Civilization** 67
   Toward a Discerning Mind and Heart / 69
   Religion as a Mechanism for Management and Control / 72
   Religion as Projection / 73
   Naming the Projections / 74
   Relational Aspirations / 76

6. **The Spirit Breaks Through** 81
   Exploring the Great Spirit / 82
   Can Christianity Accommodate the Great Spirit? / 84
   Moving beyond the Ex Nihilo *Creator* / 87
   The Spirit of Paradox / 90

7. **Artificial Intelligence and the Evolutionary Human** 93
   The Rise of AI / 94
   The Climate Emergency of the Twenty-First Century / 102
   Grounding Our Identity as Earthlings / 104
   Super-Intelligent Earthlings / 105

8. **Doing Theology in an Evolutionary Way** 109
   Tradition and Recapitulation / 110
   Confronting the Anthropocene / 113
   Creatures of a Relational Creation / 116

Works Cited 119

Index 127

Introduction

Over the centuries, Christian theology has flourished as a vision of robust faith, centered on an all-powerful God who is known and loved for the salvation this God makes possible for human beings. The doctrines of theology have focused on the mystery and meaning of God, and theology's influence has been largely determined by a particular understanding of the human condition, with the ultimate goal of saving human souls.

As a human-based enterprise, the theological landscape has changed dramatically. Particularly through the scientific study of human origins (paleoanthropology), we no longer understand the human to be a codependent sinful being. We are, rather, complex evolutionary creatures, flourishing over a time span of some seven million years.

Over long time spans, human beings have exhibited a resilient creativity, reflecting and illuminating the creativity of the Godhead itself. The mystery of human becoming opens up the mysterious meaning of God in a profoundly new way. The new horizons of our human evolutionary narrative invite us into a novel exploration of that which grounds everything in sacred meaning, the human and nonhuman alike.

In the twenty-first century, theology is embracing the enlarged wisdom arising from cosmology, evolutionary theory, quantum physics, ecology, and the new biology. Strangely, however, there seems to be little recognition of the advances being made in the field of paleoanthropology. Incorporating insights about human origins has revolutionary implications for our understanding of incarnation and God's embodied presence with humans and our ancestors throughout our entire seven million years.

Our current spiritual awakening follows an interdisciplinary trajectory and transcends much of the past dualistic split between the sacred and the secular. We are invited into the enlarged scientific horizons of our time. Particularly for the present work, we are tasked to learn from the amazing discoveries we are making in relation to our long evolutionary narrative on this earth. On several fronts, secular resources seem to be outpacing sacred learnings of the past, calling forth a spiritual exploration that can engage peoples from several wisdom traditions, some religious, others of no particular religious allegiance.

This book is for all those people who are seeking new spiritual meaning amid a decadent religious world, where inherited doctrines and dogmas lose meaning and relevance at a rapidly increasing rate. It explores how the divine Spirit still continues to renew the face of the earth, reawakening within the human spirit an organic evolutionary wisdom too long suppressed and denied.

Welcome to the exploration!

1

A Context Too Long Neglected

But whereas the origin of humans was once an uncomfortable speculation in Darwin's big idea, it is now among the best-documented examples of evolution's transformative power.
—Kate Wong

For this divinity arises out of those unruly depths, over which language catches its breath.
—Catherine Keller

Christian theology has evolved into an ever more enlarged and complex landscape in the last seventy years. Long a science based on the metaphysical certainties garnered from Greek philosophy, and reinforced by the imperial monopoly of Constantine's legacy, it enjoyed an unquestioned superiority for much of the two thousand years of Christendom. A change came around the middle of the twentieth century. The unquestioned certainties of the past began to collapse at an accelerated pace.

Moving out of the protective canopy of ecclesiastical allegiance, theology began to embrace a world that was becoming ever more fluid amid evolutionary momentum. "Rational" science had been considered to be theology's longtime secular enemy. It began to open up and illuminate the mysterious creation that we humans inhabit. In Christian theology the patriarchal, hierarchical God-above-the-Sky began to give way to a refreshing sense of sacred presence within our cosmic and earthly habitats. The long enduring dualistic split between the sacred and the secular began to disintegrate. And theology responded by becoming the new bridge builder, with what, at times, feels like a totally new provenance.

Several scholars describe such changes as a paradigm shift, the decline and death of a former model and the emergence of something that marks a significant departure from previous understandings. And yet, despite these major shifts in understanding and the promise of new possibilities, this book investigates a missing dimension with even more substantial implications. Traditionally, Christian theology predicates and predicts a major shift in the meaning of human life, offering salvation and redemption for human deliverance from all forms of human meaninglessness. That promised utopia is wearing thin and rapidly losing credibility in the modern world.

I contend that the anthropology that has been employed in dominant Christian theology is too narrow and reductionist. Essentially, it is an anthropology that is based on the cultural evolution of recent millennia and largely, if not totally, ignorant of our long evolutionary story of several previous millennia. Christian theological anthropology must come up to date by digging back, deep into questions and insights that are pursued in paleoanthropology.

Theological Change in the Twenty-First Century

To understand life in its deeper meaning, we need to embrace the multiple perspectives that constitute everything in creation. Interdisciplinary projects are gaining significance across the sciences. Nothing really makes sense in isolation, and we need to come to terms with the fact that the reality of our world is not static either. We live in a world that is interrelated and forever changing and evolving into greater complexity.

Religion and theology are embracing the wisdom of other sciences. It feels like the rigid impermeable boundaries are breaking down as refreshing waters flood in. Christian cosmo-theology explores the relationship with evolution (Haught

2010, 2015; Delio 2015, 2023). Christian liberation theology incorporates insights from Marxist theory, politics, and economics (Boff 1995; McFague 2001; Tanner 2005). Ecological concerns, like global warming, engage both theological discourse and spiritual awakening in our time (Biviano 2016; O'Murchu 2023). And even the so-called hard sciences of physics, chemistry, and biology are being reviewed for various links within our religious worldviews.

Strangely, paleoanthropology remains a science that has been scarcely recognized in theology and religion despite rigorous investigation within the field in the last forty years.[1] In general, major world religions seem to work within a human narrative of merely a few thousand years. Humans are viewed as quite a young species, with a religious significance not exceeding five thousand years. This view seems to assume that humans and our religious beliefs only make sense within the context of civilization.[2] Furthermore, this approach can lead us to assume that God also deals with our human reality in the same civilizational context.

Even in the brilliant insights of Charles Darwin into the origins of ants and armadillos, bats and barnacles, one species is conspicuously neglected in his major work, *On the Origin of Species* (1859). Regarding *Homo sapiens*, Darwin made only a passing mention on the third-to-last page of the tome, noting coyly that "light will be thrown on the origin of man and his history" (Darwin 1859, 488). That is all he wrote about the dawning of the single most consequential species on the planet.

---

[1] Different writers use various naming conventions for this science. *Paleoanthropology* is the official title for the study of human evolution. However, it is sometimes described simply as *palaeontology*, which means specifically the study of life on earth through ancient fossils.

[2] Historically, *civilization* (from the Latin *civis*, meaning "citizen," and *civitas* meaning "city") is a term applied to any society which has developed a writing system and the structures of urbanization. According to this definition, the first civilizations include the Indus Valley Civilization (c.7000–c.600 BCE), Mesopotamia's Sumerian civilization (6000–1750 BCE), and the Egyptian civilization (6000–30 BCE). Consequently, human life prior to about seven thousand years ago was considered to be uncivilized, primitive, and barbaric.

Twelve years later he published a book devoted to that very subject, *The Descent of Man*. In it, he explains that discussing humans in his earlier treatise would have served only to further prejudice readers against his radical ideas. Yet, even in this later work, he has little to say about human origins per se, instead focusing on making the case from comparative anatomy, embryology, and behavior that, like all species, humans, too, are creatures of evolution.

In Darwin's day, of course, there was hardly any fossil record to provide evidence of earlier stages of human existence than *Homo sapiens*. To his credit, Darwin made astute observations about our kind and predictions about our ancient past based on the information that was available to him. He argued that all living humans belong to one species and that its "races" all descended from a single ancestral stock. Pointing to the anatomical similarities between humans and African apes, he concluded that chimpanzees and gorillas were the closest living relatives of humans, highlighting the fact that we originally evolved out of Africa.

Every catechism ever compiled begins with basic statements about God's creation of the world, further asserting that this same creative God begets and sustains every new development in the evolutionary story of life. God is fully there and involved as each new life-form comes into being and enriches the unfolding fabric of creation at large. What, then, is the religious significance of our oldest known human ancestor, believed to have walked our earth some seven million years ago?

Was the creative God not doing a new thing when a new hominin life-form emerged some seven million years ago? If there is a divine novelty at work here, why wait till about five thousand years ago to discern and explore its spiritual, religious, and theological meaning? Why not use this ancient story, becoming ever more accessible to us in the light of current paleoanthropology, to understand more deeply the creativity of God at work in our human species today? By restricting our investigation into God at work in the human merely to recent millennia, are we playing a game of idolatry, reducing God to a cultural artifact, a projection of our human urge to dominate and control? Are we undermining the mystery and meaning of our own humanity, robbing it of the elegance and creativity of our long evolutionary narrative?

What might it mean if we adopt a kind of Buddhist transparency? Let God be God. Allow ourselves to be informed by the God who works across the ages, across evolutionary time spans that illuminate divine intent, bringing a bigger and deeper context to our human yearning for meaning and purpose in life.

Our Bankrupt Anthropology

Before we can delve more deeply into our older evolutionary story and its suggested richness for faith and theology, we need to clear away the rubble that has accumulated over recent millennia. We take as normative the anthropological paradigm of the past 5,000 years. Virtually every field of study assumes that our human ancestor of these recent millennia is significantly different from all that went before, a creature with a superior form of intelligence and capability unknown in earlier ages.

The split from the past is about a great deal more, asserting that everything that transpired in our human evolution prior to about 5,000 years ago can simply be discarded as evidence for a way of being human that was so primitive and barbaric that it has little or nothing to offer for a contemporary understanding of the human condition. Religion, more than any other field of learning, makes this claim, thus also asserting (at least implicitly) that God was up to nothing good during all those millennia—if God was involved at all.

This disturbingly negative appraisal of our human evolutionary story can be traced to about twelve thousand years ago, to an emergence known as the Agricultural Revolution.[3]

---

[3] This is a complex topic on which a great deal has been written, yet scholars are quite divided on their interpretation on what was transpiring at that time. The Agricultural Revolution is often portrayed as the rise of agriculture for the first time, through the domestication of animals and the cultivation of land for crops and food. In fact, our human species

The rise of the Agricultural Revolution is usually associated with the Levant—roughly corresponding to modern-day Israel, Jordan, Lebanon, Syria, and adjacent areas. It is possible that the greatest impact on ensuing human dislocation took place on what Steve Taylor describes as Saharasia, combining what today we identify as the desert regions of the Sahara and the Arabian Peninsula (more in Taylor 2005, 50–51, 120–24).

Prior to the southerly shift of the ice, Saharasia consisted of rich fertile plains, heavily populated by humans. Then, in what seems to have been a rather abrupt weather crisis, the fertile plains gradually became the barren deserts we know today. As we can easily imagine, this caused massive disruption and severe dislocation of human populations. A new subculture of management and frenetic control emerged out of the crisis. Over a few thousand years, land came to be seen as a commodity for humans to manage. Because land resources were now drastically reduced, human rivalries over the acquisition of land began to arise. Steve Taylor calls this period the ego-explosion. It was characterized by largely male practices of acquisition and domination that came to form patriarchal systems of human relationships (Taylor 2005, 114–29).

From a religious point of view, land became secularized, no longer perceived as a nourishing resource from a benevolent deity who, often, inhabited the land itself. God was now extracted from the land and projected to an upper cosmic realm that later came to be known as heaven. From there, God was

---

had been cultivating land for some thousands of years before this time, with women as well as men involved. British archaeologist Paul Pettitt claims: "Many of the traits that are taken to define agricultural life were present, at least in incipient form, as early as 31,000 years ago" (Pettitt 2022, 265). It seems that a number of weather patterns contributed to this new development, the more benign conditions following after the cold icy conditions that swept down across Europe, continuing southward over North Africa and east into what today is known as the Arabian desert. The last Ice Age, otherwise known as the Last Glacial Period (LGP), is usually dated between 115,000 and 11,700 years ago, and peaked around 20,000 years ago. But even as the global climate progressively warmed in the subsequent millennia, there were still long periods in which colder conditions returned. For more, see Langutt et al. 2021.

believed to be the supreme ruler, validating the governance of the ruling males on the earth. In time, this led to a new hierarchy whereby the governing God-above-the-Sky ruled down, primarily through the supreme ruler on Earth, duly called the "King."[4]

With the sociopolitical evolution of kings, two other institutional figures follow shortly thereafter: warriors and priests. The warrior denotes the rise of violence as a validated patriarchal and religious requirement for domination and control. Contemporary theologians sometimes call it redemptive violence (Camp 2023; Schwager 1987). Correspondingly, priests were equipped to offer sacrifice to appease the ruling God-above-the-Sky. The emergence of civilization followed.

Civilizations first appeared in Mesopotamia (what is now Iraq) around four thousand years ago. Civilizations thrived in the Indus Valley by about 2500 BCE and in China by about 1500 BCE. In its historical context a civilization is characterized by two features: urbanization and written language. Both urbanization and written record-keeping reinforced the patriarchal will to power and domination. Urbanization, in various contexts, contributed mightily to structures of social stratification. By modernity, urbanization is a key feature of the emerging nation-state. Until relatively recent mass-literacy campaigns, the written language served elite and bureaucratic purposes. The world's oldest known written languages, particularly Sumerian cuneiform, come down to us in the records that were kept: taxes, grocery bills, laws, and the like. Over time, the civilized world began to look ever more like our own situation today.

In a short while, classical Greek culture would emerge. Socrates, Plato, and particularly, Aristotle, are key figures for understanding Greek anthropology. The power of reason was now portrayed as the ultimate achievement of the human mind,

---

[4] Kings may have evolved as early as eight thousand years ago. Worthy of note, however, is the claim of British historian Dominic Lieven (2022) that kings are of relatively recent origin, not older than six thousand years ago. Lieven also notes that religion and kingship have been intertwined from their respective beginnings.

capable of bringing the human spirit into alignment with the mind of the supreme ruling deity. To that end, both Plato and Aristotle created a new understanding of human personhood.

Classical Greek Anthropology

For Aristotle, the human person is essentially autonomous, separate, ensouled, and rational. Ontologically, we each stand on our own. We are separate from, and superior to, all other aspects of the material creation. The soul links the human to God in a unique way. Finally, as ensouled beings, we work things out through the God-given power of reason. The Greeks sought to extricate humans from their enmeshment in the material creation, so that they could evolve into more superior beings deemed to be closer to the gods. Differentiation from our animal nature was considered to be particularly important. The rational soul is the key differentiating factor. For both Plato and Aristotle, the human soul is the seat of reason. Essentially, the rational soul makes the human person unique, for we have the ability to think things out rationally.

For Aristotle, rationality is a divine quality: "The human being is the only erect animal because its nature and essence is divine; the function of the most divine is thinking and being intelligent" (*De partibus animalium* IV.10 686a 27–29). In both the *Nichomachean Ethics* and in *De Anima*, Part 3, Aristotle writes extensively about human flourishing and the happiness (*eudaimonia*) that ensues. To use a later Christian phrase, he views the human as made in the image of God (*imago Dei*). This impressive philosophical development has been heavily endorsed by philosophers over the past two millennia.

Yet, the subtleties require closer and more discerning attention. For instance, for many of the Greek Fathers, the *imago Dei* resides in the nonsexual soul rather than the fully embodied human, and it is much more present in the man than in the woman.[5] These deviations—in the Greek Fathers and the

---

[5] This topic of the *imago Dei* is extensively reviewed by Daniel P. Horan (2019, 87ff.).

much earlier Aristotle—cannot be explained simply by situating Aristotle within the biological and cultural knowledge of his time. Christian interpretative tradition has tended to read Aristotle literally, and he still enjoys exalted status in Scholastic philosophy. Here, things have gone drastically wrong for our understanding of both God and humans.

Developing his metaphysical anthropology, Aristotle was concerned primarily with males. Females were dismissed as misbegotten males, an unfortunate demonization that St. Thomas Aquinas adopted some twelve hundred years later, a misogyny that still haunts Christianity. Aristotle's allegiance to the autonomous, robust, individualistic, and heroic male as the model for all responsible and holy humans is more demeaning than just the attention to males.[6] This same individualized sense of personhood was employed in the early Christian Councils—Nicaea, Chalcedon, Constantinople—in the deliberations about God as person. We are dealing with a set of philosophical anthropological theories that were also projected onto our understanding of God.

Today, the Aristotelian definition of the human person dictates much of our social constructions of reality in politics, economics, education, science, and religion. There are meager residues of an alternative anthropology in some of our tribal cultures and among First Nations peoples. In Africa, one occasionally still hears allusions to the notion of *Ubuntu*: "I am because we are." Contemporary anthropology and psychology occasionally seek to reinstate this subverted view of the human with the cryptic assertion that I am at all times the sum of my relationships, and this is what gives me identity (Boeve et al. 2014).

Human identity is not merely a one-off accomplishment. Rather, it is a life-long process, unfolding over time and involving a complex range of cosmic, planetary, organic, human, and spiritual influences. David G. Kirchhoffer usefully writes:

---

[6] Social system's theorist Jeremy Lent (2017) offers a valuable critical overview of Aristotelian anthropology.

> Possibly the primary challenge to theological anthropology is that 21st century theology will not be defined by who or what the human person is (the classical questions of a substance metaphysics), but by *where* in the world the person is. . . . Whereas the tradition has usually talked about the person being IN the world, the great realization of the latter half of the 20th century may indeed be that we ARE the world. We are so fundamentally bound up in an infinite network of relationships that to even conceive of some sort of objective self or human essence verges on the absurd. (Boeve et al. 2014, 185)

This is quite strong language, and it is potentially disturbing for the millions who still employ the notion of a personal God with whom we can relate interpersonally. As with many other issues arising in this book, people and cultures assume that our highly individualized understanding of human personhood has been the norm over several millennia. In fact, it is quite a recent development—little more than three thousand years old. It is yet another byproduct of the shadow side of the Agricultural Revolution, a further cultural reinforcement of imperial kingship, patriarchal power, and a hegemonic ideology that has been popularly described as civilization.

Current, highly individualized anthropologies are a betrayal of a relational understanding that flourished and developed over our long evolutionary history. Theologically, this relational understanding offers a far healthier and more integrated view of God and personhood over the seven-million-year story of hominin evolution. The rest of this chapter engages exciting questions for theological anthropology in this relational key, on such a time span.

We Are the World

Aristotle was eager to redeem humans from the enmeshment in their messy organic surroundings, distinguishing them from the rest of creation. His logic is simple: humans have a rational soul and other creatures do not. Among other consequences, the rational soul contributes to the superiority of humans over all other creatures. As rational beings, humans are separated from the rest of the natural world.

In short, Aristotle's philosophical anthropology, expectedly, lacks an attention to evolutionary becoming. The rational, separate, and autonomous human person whom Aristotle envisions is positioned to achieve a mastery over and against others: other humans and other creatures. Any sense of integral connection with our nearest kin—the primates, animals, or mammals—is largely absent in his vision of life. Today's philosophical attention to our animal nature is at quite a variance with classical Greek anthropology.[7] Sadly, it is also unrecognized by several contemporary scholars of various disciplines.

We are the World! We are of the Earth! We are Earthlings! This affirmation requires us to examine our human nature and identity within a very different context, one that may be described as that of integral wholeness.[8] The following are just some of the dimensions that will need to be considered:

1. *Our Cosmic Identity*—It is not a wild poetic streak that requires us to trace our evolving story back to the Big Bang, some 13.8 billion years ago.[9] In that generic event, the creative energy of every life-form exists in embryonic outline (cf. Swimme 2022). It becomes more visible a few billion years later as dying stars bestow on the rest of creation chemical resources like carbon and iron. Another cosmic endowment is that of sunlight, which through the process of photosynthesis, co-creates

---

[7] There are notable scholars who support this realignment with our animality in philosophy and theology, and their work is a welcome response to the perpetual insistence on our separation from the world. They include scholars such as David Abram (2010), Melanie Challenger (2021), Celia Deane-Drummond (2014), and Ed Yong (2022).

[8] Developed at great length by Franciscan theologian Ilia Delio (2023).

[9] I am not alluding to the Anthropic Principle, which basically states that the universe saw us coming and has put everything in place for us to evolve as an unique outcome of the cosmic evolutionary process. This can easily lead to another form of anthropocentric imperialism.

the nourishing potentialities that enable all life-forms, including humans, to grow and develop.
2. *Our Planetary Identity*—In and through our emergence on the earth and our close affiliation with it as earthlings, we appropriate and integrate all that makes our lives fertile, relational, and meaningful.
3. *Our Mobility*—As we came down from the trees and began to walk upright—possibly as far back as our oldest known ancestor, *Sahelanthropus tchadensis*—we manifest a capacity and desire to explore.
4. *Our Toolmaking*—Now dated to some 3.3 million years ago, our ancestors' tools reveal a quality of intelligence and creativity long considered to have been impossible before the evolution of language around 100,000 years ago.
5. *Our Cognitive Endowment*—*Homo habilis*, evolving some 2.4 million years ago, had a larger brain than previous hominins. *Homo erectus*, first evolving around 1.9 million years ago, with a brain size about 25 percent larger than that of *Homo habilis*, exhibited many indications of enhanced intelligence, creativity, and the ability to adapt to the environment, employing the use of sophisticated, task-specific, stone hand axes, complex stable seasonal home bases, and long-distance hunting strategies involving large game.
6. *The Evolution of Language*—The emergence of language is dated conservatively to around 100,000 years ago. It is believed to have been an emergent property, which, in the form of proto-language (nonverbal gestures, sounds, and so on), goes further back, over several thousand years.
7. *Our Patterning Instinct*—Largely associated with the pioneering work of social theorist Jeremy Lent, humans manifest an evolutionary propensity to seek out relational patterns that enhance our growth and development as earthlings (Lent 2017; 2021). This same relational dynamic can be observed in creation at large, exemplified in the claims of quantum mechanics.

8. *Our Spiritual Awakening*—This is usually assumed to be an endowment that followed on the evolution of formal religion about thirty-five hundred years ago. Yet, we have known for several years now that our *Homo neanderthalensis* ancestors buried their dead with elaborate ceremonies, unmistakably religious or spiritual in nature. There is no known assistance from priests or other religious specialists in these burials. While various scholars, such as E. Fuller Torrey, seek to establish belief in God on more solid scientific grounds, such research fails to explain the much older spiritual ethos that manifests in our human creative endeavors of which Ice Age art is an eminent example.[10]

9. *Ritual Makers*—David Graeber and David Wengrow highlight our capacity for ritual making with transcendent meaning as an endowment of great age (2021). Rituals related to the ancient burial of the dead date back to 100,000 years ago. In time, we are likely to find evidence indicating that the discovery of fire some one million years ago also involved ritual engagement. Our capacity for ritual making seeks expression in the sacramental systems of contemporary Christian denominations. Unfortunately, religious scholars often fail to note this fertile link.

Individuality, Relationship, and Personhood

As humans, we are intimately wrapped up in our capacity for spiritual meaning. This capacity dates back into deep time, expressed in millions of years. *Animism* is often associated with worshiping the sun, suggesting that our ancestors recognized a transcendent, beneficent resource that significantly affected their lives.

---

[10] Torrey details the neurobiological sequence that explains why the gods appeared when they did, connecting archaeological findings including clothing, art, farming, and urbanization to cognitive developments. He presents religious belief as an inevitable outcome of brain evolution (Torrey 2017).

Did they consider it to be a personal force? Probably not. The lack of personal identification has led some philosophically minded people to conclude that we are dealing with some kind of primitive instinct deprived of all sense of rational intelligence. In this regard, I suggest it is helpful to distinguish between the impersonal and the transpersonal. We tend to dismiss as *impersonal* everything that is not congruent with our inherited Aristotelian notion of the robust rational individual. The *transpersonal*, on the other hand, invites us to transcend the narrow individualistic stereotype and embrace the relational matrix out of which all beings unfold, including humans. Our coming into being and our becoming as earthlings are interwoven with all the cosmic-planetary factors outlined earlier in this chapter.

Consider the following simple exercise. Stretch out your hands to right and left as far as you can, thus creating a stretch of approximately one meter to both your left and right. You are now experiencing yourself as an energy being, since each of us as embodied creatures are surrounded by various fields of energy that stretch out to approximately one meter from our physical bodies. Next, become aware of two selves and not merely one. With your hands resting at your side, you are engaging with your physical, material body. With your hands stretched out, you are engaging with your energy body. Both are real, ultra-real, but the more real of the two is actually your energy body. This is what keeps you connected with the wider web of life and provides organic resources that are essential to your growth and development. At the end of your earthly existence, your physical, material body will cease, but the energy body, like all forms of energy, will reconnect with other forms of energy and continue to flourish in another energy context—not in another world, but *within* this cosmic creation!

Now, we are approaching the deep meaning of human personhood, understood as a transpersonal process. In the evolving process of creation we humans are events rather than static, physical beings. We can mark the beginning and end of our physical lives, but our energy selves continue indefinitely. We are forever interconnecting.

What, then, does individual identity as persons mean? It is worth remembering that everything that operates within and around our bodies is given to us from the larger universe. Trees provide a helpful example. When we look at an individual tree, we view it as different from all others. Externally, it is. We assume that the life vitality of the tree is inherited from its roots, which beget the sap, traveling up through each tree to produce the trunk, leaves, flowers, and fruits.

This is quite a naive understanding and, in fact, is largely false. The roots are essential to the existence of a tree and always will be. Roots, though, contribute only in a minimal way to the growth and development of a tree. Trees constitute open systems. They are not closed, relying largely on their respective roots. As an open system, the tree is an interdependent process that relies heavily on the nourishing potential of photosynthesis, mediated through sunlight, water, air, and a range of chemicals that are bestowed by the surrounding environment. *Every tree is a relational organism rather than an individual entity.*

Suzanne Simard is a leading world authority on a field of research belonging very much to the opening decades of the twenty-first century: silvology.[11] She has studied and identified the intricate processes whereby trees in a forest, through their root systems, are often facilitating processes of communication that enable the trees to renew and flourish. In the forest life, the roots serve interconnection and interdependence and not merely the individual identity of a particular tree. Individuality is real in both the case of the tree and the human person, but it serves a dynamic greater than itself. Individuality enhances a quality and quantity of relationship that cannot be explained at merely the observable or rational level.

The End of Dogmatism

Today, the sciences are being lured into a more relational mode of perception, understanding, and operation. Interdisciplinary

---

[11] See Simard 2021. Other relevant names are those of Tristan Gooley (2023) and Peter Wohlleben (2023).

research and multi-disciplinary analysis is on the rise, particularly in higher education. The dogmatic rigidity and certainty of the past no longer delivers meaning for an ever-increasing number of people. A similar development is discernible in both religion and theology.

For American process theologian Catherine Keller, theology has been growing uncertain for centuries; therein lies its greatest opportunity (Keller 2003). This is something of an overstatement but worthy of our attention. Dogmatic "certainty" within the Christian tradition only came to the fore in the fourth century, largely under the influence of Constantine's imperialism. Prior to that time, theology, it seems, was a very fluid, exploratory enterprise. It took shape through the creative interactions of ordinary people (more in Vearncombe et al. 2022). In Latin Christianity, theology lost much of its imperial, rational supremacy and began to flourish alongside the mystical and ecological spirituality of the Early Middle Ages.

Perhaps the greatest rigidity of all happened in the sixteenth century when the Catholic Church through the Council of Trent (1545–63), sought to establish a robust doctrinal system that would ensure that nothing like the Protestant Reformation could ever happen again. Paradoxically, the Protestant reformers adopted a similar rigidity, seeking to develop "authentic truth" through an ever more literalist approach to scripture and church observance.[12] That ecclesiastical rigidity, and an accompanying trend toward reinforcing legalism (as in canon law), lasted well into the twentieth century and has been progressively unravelling ever since then.

However, at another level, Catherine Keller's observation is spot on. Apart from the ecclesiastical momentum over Christianity's two thousand years, there has been a consistent and parallel counterculture, an alternative wisdom from the ground up, that has questioned the supremacy of formal teaching, proposed alternative visions of faith, and in many cases, paid the ultimate price for such prophetic audacity, as

---

[12] Inadvertently, both movements were influenced by the emergence of rational Newtownian science around that same time.

in the Inquisition of the eleventh through eighteenth centuries. That alternative wisdom has been gaining greater influence since 1960. It will continue to exert major influence for the foreseeable future.

The interface of theology with several other sciences as noted in the paradigm shifts above has created a culture of uncertainty that today is often named postmodernism. Former dogmatic certitude has lost an enormous amount of influence, and, in several cases, it has created a fundamentalist backlash from those who are still committed to the imperial paradigm. That polarization is likely to continue well into the twenty-first century and is also evident in politics, social policy, and economics. It will neither halt nor undermine theology's expansive stretch, however, as long as theology continues to be guided by the Spirit, who blows where it wills.

That same Spirit has been weaving waves of creative possibility since the dawn of time. Our human attempt to honor and reclaim that Spirit-infused creative energy—over long eons past—inspires the present work. Some theologians are already realigning theology with the new cosmology, dating back some 13.8 billion years. Others are engaging the earth story of some four billion years. This book focuses on a much more reduced timescale, namely, the seven million years of hominin evolution.

Paleoanthropology tells the story of human origins through rigorous science, yet its insights have not seeped into our contemporary human consciousness. As we continue to pursue the meaning of human personhood, learning from paleoanthropology has the potential to change our ways of experiencing our significance in the world in enormous ways. We must learn to be—and then actually become—better relatives with our fellow humans and with all other creatures. It is to be hoped that the wisdom garnered here raises our awareness to the possibilities for flourishing lives for ourselves and for all other life-forms.

2

Our Human Story and Divine Revelation

Cut off in its earliest stage, dammed up close to its source, our instinctive empathy with the earthly surroundings remains stunted in most contemporary persons.

—David Abram

Two things fill my mind with ever-increasing wonder and awe, the more often and the more intensely the reflection dwells on them: the starry heavens above me and the moral law within me.

—Immanuel Kant

In Christian terms the human story begins with the opening chapter of Genesis. The Genesis stories describe a human situation through the lens of the Agricultural Revolution. In the first of the two different creation stories in Genesis, God called humans "good" along with every other creature throughout creation. In the second creation story, however, the plot turns sour. In that story God creates humanity from the dust of the earth and places humans in a garden. Though agricultural, there are clear messages about the goodness of relationships among the humans, all of creation, and God. From that garden, God, humans, and all creatures become enmeshed in ever-increasing violence and destruction as humanity distorts and breaks its relationships.

The two stories in Genesis are not competing with each other. The first story is actually the younger of the two, and it is poetic. It is a way of telling the human story within rituals that were important to the Hebrew communities who wrote the scriptures. As I noted in the previous chapter, we humans are ritual makers. This first Genesis story is an example of how a group of humans used Agricultural Revolution language about the human person to make sense of their humanity in ceremonies with transcendent meaning. The second story, the older story, is also in the frame of the Agricultural Revolution. It starts out with humans as a part of creation in the garden and ends with humans apart from creation by being expelled from the garden. The Fall, as it has been called, is a result of humans distorting their relationships with other creatures and God to the breaking point. Those relationships, though, were still based in the instructions that God gave to humans to till and keep the garden, suggesting that agricultural subsistence was a human responsibility. In the end, the humans' relational break became such a problem that it has been inherited down the generations.

Christian Salvation

The Genesis stories are powerful and foundational myths![1] Christian visions of humanity, especially in Latin traditions like Roman Catholicism and Protestantism, have read these stories as allegorically true and historic fact at different times

---

[1] Throughout this book I use the notion of myth to denote a type of narrative that occurs transculturally in our human search for meaning, stories that cannot be dismissed as fictional tales or superstitious legends, but rather are highly symbolic narratives into which we are drawn intellectually and emotionally, both consciously and subconsciously. When a myth is working, it creates an idealized picture seeking a worldview that is relatively coherent, harmonious, sensible, and therefore meaningful, so that life seems worth living. Although somewhat dated, the short and comprehensive overview of the renowned anthropologist Claus Levi-Strauss (d.1992) is still valuable (Levi-Strauss 1978). For the general reader, I recommend McIntosh (2004).

in history. With the rise of biological evolutionary theory, many fundamentalist theologians and preachers have used these texts to promote theological stories about humanity that reinforce our violent separation from other creatures and our autonomy as persons and a species. Even when scholars have disputed the way that these stories are used to ground theories of original sin, the anthropological commitments often continue (O'Murchu 2018).

The anthropology that we have inherited from interpretations of these stories down through the centuries is multifaceted. Some cultures or Christian communities emphasize different elements of our inherited anthropology more than others. First, the narrative of a fall assumes that humanity was created in an initial, original state of perfection. In this state, humans coexisted in harmonic innocence with one another and all of creation. Given what we now know about evolutionary biology, this story has no factual basis. Rather than communicate facts about the world, this theological anthropological element prioritizes a vision of humanity as originally created to be perfect alongside a perfectly omnipotent God without ever being gods ourselves. Second, the Fall itself is interpreted as a fall away from our rightful place alongside this omnipotent God because we sought out equality with God in the garden. Third, now that we are fallen, humans try to obtain, hoard, and retain power to control whenever and however we can. We battle ourselves, one another, and our world in attempts to reclaim what we thought was "perfect" power. In the previous chapter I referenced Steve Taylor's work, in which he calls this the "ego-explosion." Humans seek to become the superior species and seek to control everything. Fourth, our preoccupation with power-to-control means that pride and disobedience become the primary sins in the human problem. They remain as major moral infringements today in patriarchal religions. Fifth, related to these sins, the dichotomy between power and powerlessness drives personal, political, and moral relationships. Power is misconstrued and misapplied as power-to-control, and powerlessness is exploited as weakness. Both the powerful and powerless become suppressed from realizing the fuller potential of their God-given humanity. These are five facets of our inherited anthropology, and they have cast humans as stuck in a profound and universal predicament.

For Christianity, Jesus is the solution to the universal human problem. Jesus's saving work is for everybody, not merely for Christians. In many Christian stories of atonement, Jesus is sent to resolve the dilemma of human sin and achieves the breakthrough by becoming the supreme victim, dying on the cross for the salvation of humanity. Despite this unique divine intervention, Christianity itself has contributed significantly to meaningless suffering in the world.

Our Sacred Human Narrative

For most people in the Euro-American West, our inherited anthropology is very much wrapped up in the Christian myth of sin and redemption. Even for non-Christians, the narrative has been dysfunctional and has seriously undermined the deeper meaning of our evolutionary growth and development. Both the cultural influence of the ancient Greeks and the moralistic perceptions of the Christian religion leave us with several serious liabilities, the suppression of our evolutionary story being the most serious of all. The fact that we have operated out of this paradigm for over two thousand years must not excuse us from probing more deeply. We need a reset that honors our evolutionary human story as God's story for us over seven million years.

In 1959, husband-and-wife paleoanthropologists Mary and Louis Leakey came across the remnants of a human skull while searching for animal and primate fossils in northwestern Tanzania.[2] Mary Leakey painstakingly extracted it from the layer of rock where it was found, and the geologists who were accompanying the expedition advised that the layer of

---

[2] The scientific search for human origins can be traced back to the closing decades of the nineteenth century, gaining ever new momentum from 1960 onward. For the earlier exploration, and some of the key people involved, see the readable and informed account of the BBC broadcaster Lucy Moore (2022).

rock in question was two million years old. Consequently, the human remains found there must have existed two million years ago.

The Leakeys themselves were baffled by the discovery. Even they were inadvertently influenced by the notion that humans belonged to quite a young species. When they challenged the geologists about that ancient date, the geologists insisted that they were in no doubt about the veracity of their claim. The Leakeys' doubts were warranted because, apart from a write-up in *National Geographic* in September 1960, they encountered a great deal of skepticism among the international scientific community. They did not succeed in having their findings published until 1964.

Until the 1940s, most anthropologists believed that humans had evolved in Asia, not in Africa. In 1891, an excavation team led by Eugène Dubois uncovered a tooth, a skullcap, and a thighbone at Trinil, on the banks of the Solo River in Eastern Java. Dubois named the species *Anthropopithecus erectus,* arguing that the fossils represented the "missing link" between apes and humans. Similar fossils were not discovered in Africa until the 1920s. In 1924, Raymond Dart's research team discovered a childlike skull, scientifically described in 1925 as *Australopithecus africanus* and popularly known as Taung Child. Several contemporary scholars dismissed the finding as a fake until Robert Broom, a Scottish doctor who trained as a paleontologist, found the first adult *Paranthropus* fossil at the Sterkfontein site in 1936.

These remain significant historical discoveries. In the latter half of the twentieth century, due in tremendous part to the work of the Leakeys, paleoanthropology gathered rapid momentum. The Leakeys led a team of scientists who discovered a fossil at the Olduvai Gorge in 1960 that was subsequently named *Homo habilis* (the handy person) in 1964. *Homo habilis* is believed to be the earliest member of the genus *Homo,* which evolved at least 2.5 million years ago.[3] *Homo habilis*

---

[3] In 2013, a fragment of fossilized jawbone was discovered in the Ledi-Geraru research area in the Afar depression of Ethiopia. The fossil—LD 350–1—seems to be an intermediate between *Australopithecus*

is the first species for which we have positive evidence for the use of stone tools. These tools represent a breakthrough that is known as Oldowan lithic technology, named after the Olduvai Gorge in which the first specimens of the tools were found. In highlighting this feature of *Homo habilis*, I am making my first allusion to the innate human capacity for *creativity*, the controversial claim of Kenneth Oakley's 1949 *Man the Tool-maker* and confirmed on much more rigorous scientific basis by Renfrew et al. (2009) and by Dietrich Stout (2016). This creative giftedness is not some primordial flaw. Rather, it characterizes our human evolutionary story, dating back to at least three million years ago.

Homo habilis, therefore, should not be understood as the first to manifest human utilitarian skills, making tools for some human function or task. There is a great deal more at stake here, unearthing the human will to co-create, the creative urge that creation itself has bestowed upon the human who, in turn, will push the creative potential to a more sophisticated and liberating level. We return to this topic in Chapter 4 below.

Next, we encounter *Homo erectus*, the oldest known early human to have possessed modern human-like body proportions, with relatively elongated legs and shorter arms compared to the size of the torso. These features are considered adaptations to a life lived on the ground, indicating the loss of earlier tree-climbing adaptations, having now acquired the ability to walk and possibly run long distances. In 2013, research was published in the journal *Science* (October 18, 2013) that describes a new male skull discovered at the Dmanisi site (D4500) in Georgia that is, very likely, a variant of the African *Homo erectus* and dated to be older than the Turkana Boy, at around 1.8 million years ago.

Homo erectus was the primordial explorer and is considered to be the first *Homo* species to have expanded beyond Africa. Fossil evidence is spread over three continents, including sites in Java and China. While *Homo habilis* probably remained

---

and *H. habilis*. It has been dated to around 2.8 million years ago, making it the earliest known evidence of the genus *Homo*.

close to base, doing whatever creative activities stonework allowed, *Homo erectus* pushed the boundaries of curiosity and ingenuity. *Homo erectus* began to sense the vastness and complexity of creation, seemingly endowed with an intuitive sense that this was raw material for human use and cleverness.

Next comes the species named as *Homo ergaster*, based on the skull of a mature adult that lived about 1.75 million years ago in Koobi Fora, Kenya. The discovery was made in 1975 by fossil hunter Bernard Ngeneo. Not only did *Homo ergaster* resemble modern humans in body structure, paleoanthropologists believe that it was more advanced in organizational skills and sociality than other earlier species. The most complete individual fossil of this species is known as the Turkana Boy (KNM-WT 15000). It is a well-preserved skeleton, though it is missing almost all the hand and foot bones. It was discovered in 1984 by Kamoya Kimeu, a member of a team led by Richard Leakey, at Nariokotome, near Lake Turkana in Kenya. The fossil has been dated to around 1.5–1.6 million years old. While it is conceivable that *Homo ergaster* was the first hominin to harness fire, it is now assumed that *Homo erectus* did have control of fire, as did other hominins sharing a common ancestry.

Most contemporary scholars believe that *Homo ergaster* emerged from *Homo erectus*, with essentially the same characteristics and capabilities. In their insights I detect a deepening evolutionary significance that has substantial implications for our expanded Christian understanding of incarnation. *Homo ergaster* bears witness to a deeper integration of three key capabilities: creative potential, an urge for innovation, and a growing sensibility to the giftedness of the living earth itself. The sacred is at work but not yet at a conscious level!

The origin of *Homo sapiens* continues to be a hotly debated subject. Many researchers still favor the evidence based on a 195,000 year old fossil from the Omo 1 site in Ethiopia. Others favor the Florisbad Skull from South Africa that has been dated to around 259,000 years ago. The fossils found at Jebel Irhoud in Morocco are, perhaps, the most promising of all. A study published in 2017 updated the dating of the

Jebel Irhoud fossils and nearby tools, bones, and charcoal to 300,000 years ago. The Jebel Irhoud material consists mainly of skulls, jaws, and teeth and is from a site also reputed for advanced stone tools.

Sapiens denotes wisdom, *the wise species*. Not to be confused with some unique brain development, the wisdom referred to here is the awareness and understanding that evolves as earthlings engage the living earth itself and learn to live with it in a convivial, befriending way (Renfrew et al. 2009). Despite the fact that life would have been raw and brutal at times, *Homo sapiens* knew how to read the earth's deeper organicity, engaging creation with a growing sense of mutual collaboration.

For contemporary humans, our ancestors in our *Homo sapiens* species are a relational base that modern anthropology has yet to recognize. First documented in the journal *Nature* (January 1987), geneticist Rebecca Cann and her research collaborators have argued for an original common hypothetical mother, dubbed *Mitochondrial Eve*. Their argument supports the claims that all modern humans originated in, and subsequently moved out from, Africa during a time span of 99,000 to 148,000 years ago. This has been called the "Out of Africa" hypothesis. Despite counterclaims of both a scientific and religious nature, Cann's theory continues to evoke corroborative support (Oppenheimer 2003).

While allowing for a degree of diversity suggested by the multiregional hypothesis, Mitochondrial Eve as a common ancestor suggests that we all evolved from one stock, with Africa as our common ancestral home. Whereas today we emphasize what makes us different, for most of our time on this earth the commonalities we shared defined our status as earthlings. In a word, the evidence for mutuality and interrelationality may be quite old, long predating the cultural differences and religious distinctions we cherish today.

These four breakthroughs—*Homo habilis*, *Homo erectus*, *Homo ergaster*, and *Homo sapiens*—mark an undeniable progression in innovation, creativity, and exploration, important signals of Holy Wisdom at work in the evolutionary story of our species. These species are the youngest emergences in the old story of human evolution. In the 1970s, Ethiopia emerged as the hot spot of paleoanthropology as fossil AL288-1 was unearthed. Famously known as Lucy in the English-speaking world, it is the most complete fossil member of the species *Australopithecus afarensis*. Lucy was found by an American researcher, Donald Johanson, in the Hadar, a remote Middle Awash region of northern Ethiopia. This area would be the location of many new hominin fossils, such as *Ardipithecus ramidus* (ARA-VP-6/500, also known as Ardi). Many of these older discoveries belong to the 1990s, under the pioneering endeavors of the UC–Berkeley researcher Tim D. White and his team, including Owen Lovejoy and Yohannes Haile-Selassie.

Entering Deep Time

Our oldest ancestor is known today from a fossil cranium that was discovered in 2001 by a French team led by Michel Brunet. Fossil TM 266-01-060-1 is better known as Toumaï. The scientific name for this ancestor is *Sahelanthropus tchadensis*, and it was discovered in Chad, more than fifteen hundred miles to the west of the rich archaeological zones in Kenya and Ethiopia. Radiometric dating has suggested a dating for the fossil as early as seven million years ago. Though we only have a skull for this ancient ancestor, scholars have been able to identify several unexpected features that belong to a line of human evolution that is distinct from our relatives among the Great Apes like chimpanzees and bonobos. The fossil exhibits tantalizing clues for its closer affinity to the human stock, and today it is deemed to be the oldest human ancestor thus far discovered.[4]

Three features in particular identify the transition to what we could describe as genuine humanity: the ability to walk upright; a brain size with a cranial capacity ranging from about 950 to 1800 cubic centimeters (modern humans average about

---

[4] While the majority of researchers concur on the originality and reliability of Toumaï (based on a single skull), some have raised reservations, as outlined in the *Journal of Human Evolution* 149 (December 2020), 1028982898.

1400 cubic centimeters); and the ability to engage creatively with stone technology. The Toumaï skull shows unambiguous evidence for upright walking based on the position of the hole where the spinal cord connects to the brain, the foramen magnum. As of 2015, the oldest evidence for stone technology comes from Kenya (East Africa) and is dated at 3.3 million years ago. Brain size has varied considerably over the eons, from 600 cubic centimeters in *Homo habilis* up to 1250 cubic centimeters in early *Homo sapiens*. Both of these are notably larger than the 320–380 cubic centimeter brain size of Toumaï.

Contemporary studies in anthropology and paleontology still fall foul of the human tendency to project onto our ancient ancestors those behaviors we dislike in ourselves as our lives unfold today. In the popular press, words like *primitive, barbaric, savage, undeveloped*, and *uncivilized* are still frequently used with qualitative baggage. Closer examination of the substantial evidence arising from contemporary research points us in a very different direction (Renfrew et al. 2009). The more we unravel our deep, ancient story, the more we encounter ancestors who were highly creative, innovative, adaptive, and at home with the earth. And as we embark upon the *Homo sapiens* stage—and perhaps also in the *Homo neanderthalensis*—we encounter ancestors using fire, evolving language, ritualizing the burial of the dead, exploring art, and traveling the seas (Renfrew and Boyd 2016). Progressively, we engage the fertility of the land and the symbolic capacity of the human mind while co-creating a range of complex social behaviors.

The Human Narrative as a Faith Story

In a previous book I made the provocative suggestion that while we humans remain very close to the earth, we flourish in several significant ways (O'Murchu 2008). The more we discern how our ancestors relate with the living earth itself, the less evidence we find for anything approaching notions of original sin; neither do we find any compelling evidence for violence and warfare until a mere few thousand years ago. We actually seem to get living well in our interrelationality right most of the time. These moments bear out Matthew Fox's perceptive insight that we humans are, first and foremost, the beneficiaries of an original blessing rather than the victims of an original sin (Fox 1983).

We are *earthlings* to the core of our being. For the first time ever, in 2015, Pope Francis declared and affirmed that same earth-centered identity: "Nature cannot be regarded as something separate from ourselves or as a mere setting in which we live. *We are part of nature*, included in it and thus in constant interaction with it" (*Laudato Si'*, no. 139, emphasis added).

We were born out of God's dreams as earthlings. If we understood our evolutionary story in a more responsible and creative way, we would see that our intimate bond with the earth itself constitutes our holiness, our sacredness in every sense. Moreover, there is growing paleontological and anthropological evidence to suggest that, the closer we remain to the earth, the more we grow and flourish to our own benefit and to the advantage of all that surrounds us. In a word, the closer we remain to the natural world, a greater likelihood prevails that we get right—in every sense!

The major problem that we must confront is our history of dualistic splitting: earth v. heaven, body v. soul, and matter v. spirit. Perceiving the world and thinking back upon it in strict binaries like these emerged as a forceful pattern in the wake of the Agricultural Revolution and became a cultural norm during the classical Greek period.[5] Such binary splitting is unknown to *Homo sapiens* for over 95 percent of our human

---

[5] This is not a claim that we have always gotten it right and only gotten it wrong for the first time after the Agricultural Revolution of some twelve thousand years ago. Being creatures of freedom, with an impulsive drive toward creativity, of course we get it wrong, probably on a frequent basis. However, our closeness to the earth provides a symbiotic corrective safeguard calling us back to more congruent behavior. What that might mean becomes much clearer when we study the life experiences of naturalists, contemporary or ancient. For the present work, I recommend David Abram's impressive autobiographical narrative, *Becoming Animal* (Abram 2010).

evolutionary story; when we account for all of our ancestors, the last twelve thousand years are minuscule.

From the perspective of human existence in our evolutionary story, *original sin* is not a foundational truth but a deceptively dangerous and seductive heresy. Furthermore, it has been morphed into dominating myths like that of "Man the Hunter," which, according to Hart and Sussman, developed from a basic Christian anthropological ideology of humans being inherently evil, aggressive, and natural killers (Hart and Sussman 2005). When we foreground this lie, we then end up subverting our long affiliation with the living earth as gatherers rather than hunters, horticulturalists rather than avid meat-eaters.

We will never get an authentic answer to the bewildering question *Where did it all go wrong?* but, at this juncture, I want to highlight two deviations that have contributed to our imbalance. First, the commodification of the earth itself is a process that can be dated back some twelve thousand years. Second, philosophical dualism that was inherited mainly from classical Greek philosophy has contributed to the antagonistic and violent anthropology that we have inherited. For humans, the consequences have been disastrous and continue to be so, leading to an ensuing set of tragic dislocations. We humans are uprooted, disempowered, and alienated.

In the words of naturalist David Abram, "An addled and anesthetized numbness is spreading rapidly through our species" (Abram 2010, 309). In this context we can understand original sin as a deviation, initially introduced by voraciously patriarchal human beings, rather than as the result of some form of divine influence. Therefore, it is up to humans to sort out the mess that we ourselves have created. Invoking a substitute divine scapegoat to rescue us through the power of the cross constitutes a massively irresponsible human "cop out" and turns God and Jesus into a blasphemous human projection.

In itself, our human evolutionary story does not prove the existence of God as the supreme divine being who is envisaged by mainline Christian theology. To the contrary, it seriously undermines the anthropocentric notion of a kind of super-human, transcendent God that is espoused by many people of many religious traditions. Our evolutionary narrative also undermines the several human projections that value omnipotence, omniscience, and other so-called perfections as necessary for divinity. Instead, in our evolutionary story we encounter a sacred life-force that is insinuated in the cosmic creation itself, luring forth a range of life-forms, becoming ever more complex and mysterious, including in our own evolutionary processes for the last seven million years.[6]

Our elegant evolutionary story provides compelling evidence for a quality of sacredness at work in all creation, uniquely so in us as the most recent human evidence for that creativity. This is not the personal God of Christian faith. It is a sacred presence with a compelling and persuasive sense of engagement that impacts profoundly on all we are and all we seek to achieve. While not being a personal being as conventionally understood, neither is it a cold impersonal force devoid of meaning and intimacy. To the contrary, it evokes a sense of meaning that is *transpersonal* and not *merely* personal.

The stumbling block here is our inherited sense of human personhood. It seems that, for much of the long evolutionary eons of our time on the earth, we have lived in a relational, convivial sense of being human, interdependently related with all other beings and deeply grounded in the earth itself. For Plato and Aristotle, this was a primitive status that was unbecoming of ensouled beings. Wes Howard-Brook notes this crucial difference between the classical Greek vision and a biblical vision of humanity, writing, "The biblical sense of the human being as earthly soil suffused with God's Spirit was replaced by a Platonic and Stoic sense of the rational mind reining in the animalistic body" (Howard-Brook 2010, 473).

---

[6] I am not in any way suggesting that we are the pinnacle of God's creation, beyond which there will be no further evolution of life. Long known as the anthropic principle, it is a claim for human superiority and species' exceptionalism that no longer makes scientific or religious sense. To the contrary, we are not the end of the evolutionary line—more complex creatures will transcend us in due course.

We must seek a return to "the animalistic body," to the cosmic and earthly context out of which humans evolved in the first place. That embodied, incarnational endeavor long predates the anthropology of classical Greek times, which, unfortunately, took on a cultural and religious significance that has undermined rather than advanced humanity's place and meaning in creation.

Christian theology has long cherished the notion that we humans are uniquely formed in the image and likeness of God, the *imago Dei*. Daniel Horan's work is particularly valuable today (Horan 2019, 87ff.). As created in the *imago Dei*, we manifest the reality of God in the world above and beyond all other creatures. In other words, God's revealing of God's self is more transparent and fulfilled in humans than in any other creature.

This divinely sanctioned anthropology is very much a by-product of our post-Agricultural evolution (the past twelve thousand years), as we began to master everything in creation and created patriarchal, imperial structures that birthed God-Himself as a ruling Deity-above-the-Sky. We put God outside the material creation. Over a few thousand years, we did not grow into the image and likeness of God. Rather, we created God in our own image and likeness, seriously undermining all sacredness in human creatures and throughout creation. This move was completed in a tragic severing when, eventually, we postulated the soul as the one and only dimension of our humanity that truly belongs to God.

By evolving such an anthropocentric "theology," we robbed ourselves and God of the magnificent unfolding of Spirit-energy in our long evolutionary story. Deeply immersed in the earth itself and befriending our unfolding as earthlings, God was weaving a different kind of revelation, a more intricate, earth-centered patterning instinct that was congruent with how the energizing Spirit works throughout the entire creation, cosmic and planetary alike. That earth-bound revelation now invites us into a whole new theological exploration that substantially changes the very meaning of the Godhead itself.

3

God's Chosen Earthlings

The misconception which has haunted philosophic literature throughout the centuries is the notion of "independent existence." There is no such mode of existence; every entity is to be understood in terms of the way it is interwoven with the rest of the universe.
—Alfred North Whitehead

In a thoroughly palpable sense, we are born of this planet, our attentive bodies coevolved in rich and intimate rapport with the other bodily forms—animals, plants, mountains, rivers—that compose the shifting flesh of this breathing world.
—David Abram

Our search for human meaning remains seriously truncated and even ossified. Our contemporary world still operates out of a prevailing paradigm that is far more insidious to our relational well-being than most people assume. Some of the underlying presuppositions that fuel this paradigm include a denigration of pre–Agricultural Revolution humanity, disproportionate elevation of so-called formal religion, predominance of Christian notions of original sin within and beyond Christianity, assumption of innate violence in humans, misunderstanding of death as both punishment and gateway to escapist fantasies, and narrow focus on present precarity without attention to broader narratives of meaning.

The prevailing paradigm that thrives on our isolation from one another also depends on a narrative that, beyond five thousand years ago, our ancestors were primitive, brutish, pre-logical, and living largely out of animal instinct. They were pre-civilized, and this has been commonly understood as uncivilized. Be clear: these adjectives are used to deny a quality of life to humans and our ancestors who lived outside of the current structures of our world. In this dominant paradigm of interpreting human history, the emergence of formal religion is perceived to be a strategy of divine rescue of the primitive humans.

We are told that it is within formalized religion that humans can find our "true" identity. We inherit this story about humans today whether we are particularly religious or not. Although only Christianity has a formal teaching on original sin, its imperialistic reach has shaped general assumption that the human has somehow fallen from the grace of our original creation, thus becoming primitive. The formal religion is then able to purport various remedies for this fundamental flaw. The dominant anthropological paradigm further argues that this flaw is expressed in humans through an innate violence. We will always be "at war" with one another, economically, interpersonally, and on broad sociocultural scales. Richard Dawkins's notion of the selfish gene is widely accepted as the genetic base for such rivalry and violence even though it is not true.

Despite the cultural advances of the past five thousand years, human destiny remains precarious and unpredictable. The contamination of original sin still dominates the human landscape. Many cultures (not just religions) see death as the ultimate cost of being fundamentally flawed, yet, paradoxically, death offers a sense of hope and meaning with the promise of fulfillment in a life hereafter. This escapist fantasy deepens present divisions between the human person and the whole of creation and amplifies the doomed-to-violence narratives mentioned above. Although the concept of human evolution has long been established in the sciences, humans generally give scant attention to larger narratives of meaning. Attention to survival and quality of life are valuable, for there is no way to respond to threats of injustice and oppression without valuing life. The preoccupation with survival in the inherited anthropology, however, is woven together with a terrifying obsession with progress in the here and now. Wedding survival and progress has further strengthened imperial expressions of power over other humans and other creatures with claims that progress is both necessary and good.

We, then, become fixated on our pursuit of the next best thing with little regard for the world that currently exists and the deep stories of creation that give millions of years of meaning to the present. Thus, making money and accruing material comfort and security continue to be the leading elements in the human search for meaning. Ultimately, exploration of our human story beyond five thousand years ago becomes perceived as an academic luxury for people who either cannot or do not wish to face the reality of who and what we are: selfish consumers and violent hoarders who need to be fixed. The formal religions, claiming access to authentic revelations of truth, end up supporting both this time context and the resulting maladaptation of humanity to the violence of our current paradigm.

These are deeply uncomfortable truths with which most of us cannot live, so we will find a range of different ways to ignore them, disown them, or explain them away. Academics, including religious specialists, spend a great deal of time rationalizing the human predicament. The perception of academic luxury as inquiry for people who do not want to deal with the "real world" is actually a lie. Academic cultural analysis is not a luxury in and of itself. It is a luxury when it has been distorted into a commodity to defend the violent, selfish autonomy and ensouled rationalism of the prevailing anthropological paradigm.

Most people in our world, including professional academics, struggle to live from one day to the next. This is the valuable priority of survival and quality of life that I mention above. Many of these people cannot afford the "commodity" called academic cultural analysis that is sold in our inherited paradigm. Instead, our deep evolutionary story reveals eons of relationality that undermine the ways that the inherited paradigm has attached survival to progress and then defined "good progress" through its fixation on money and material wealth. We human beings are meaning-seeking creatures, consistently pursuing and making meaning of, in, and through our world. We have inherited an anthropological paradigm that actively constricts the context in which we search for meaning. Currently, our search is too narrow and reductionist precisely because the broader and more complex search would shatter deeply held narratives about ourselves, the cosmos, and God as isolated and self-contained entities. As spiritual beings in a Spirit-endowed creation, our more authentic selves need a larger landscape.

Earthlings at Home in Creation

Thus far, I have been arguing that, as a species, we need to reclaim and inhabit afresh our true evolutionary story, embracing our seven-million-year emergence. From a faith perspective, I boldly stand by the belief that the creativity of the divine life-force, by whatever name we choose, has been with us throughout that entire time, blessing us with a quality of flourishing and meaning that we have scarcely begun to understand.

I now move my argument forward, engaging another feature of our long evolutionary story that has not been duly acknowledged and appropriated. We are *earthlings*. We are creatures that, as Abram says above, "compose the shifting flesh of this breathing world." Whether climbing trees or roaming the savannahs of East Africa, our entire seven-million-year story has been an earth-centered narrative. In and through our earthly corporeality, we became the creative beings that our God desired us to become. Without a meaningful immersion in that same earth, we cannot hope to evolve meaningfully into future possibilities. Without an embracing and nurturing the earth, we would never have made it through, nor could we have evolved the unique creative potentials that characterize us as an earth species. We are earthlings. It is all we are and everything we are.

Naturalist David Abram captures something of that intricate earth-grounding when he writes:

> The feelings that move us—the frights and yearnings that colour our days, the flights of fancy that sometimes seize us, the creativity that surges through us—all are born of the ongoing interchange between our life and the wider Life that surrounds us. They are no more ours than they are Earth's. They blow through us, and often change us, but they are not our private possession, nor an exclusive property of our species. With the other animals, as with the crinkled lichens and the river-carved rocks, we are all implicated within this intimate and curiously infinite world. (Abram 2010, 157–58)

Our becoming as earthlings constitutes two determining factors: our cosmic and planetary dimensions. They are intricately insinuated in all we are and will become. First, we are the beneficiaries of a cosmic evolutionary process that is intimately interwoven with several of the basic features of our daily lives:

> The water in your body contains primordial hydrogen formed in the first seconds of the Big Bang. The carbon atoms that formed you came together after the explosion of a supernova. The concentration of salt in your body matches the concentration of salt in the ancient seas. Your cells are direct descendants of unicellular organisms that developed billions of years ago. You see because chlorophyll molecules mutated, so that like plant leaves, your eyes can capture the light from the sun. And in your mother's womb your tiny body repeated the whole process of multi-cellular life on earth, beginning with a single

cell, and then developing greater and greater complexity. (Cannato 2006, 65)[1]

Our corporeal identity is that of sun energy, stardust, and the interwoven complexity of several energy forces belonging to the vast womb of our evolving universe. I do not support the anthropic principle, claiming that creation has been waiting for us to evolve as the supreme organic life form. Rather, we are one of a vast range of evolutionary life-forms, articulating the creative potential of the universe. Each is unique, but none is superior.

What we receive from the vast universe is substantial and essential to the health and development of our daily lives. However, none of such beneficence would be ours without the mediation of the earth body within which we are intimately interwoven. British scientist Lewis Dartnell writes:

> I want to explore how the Earth made us. The water in your body once flowed down the Nile, fell as monsoon rain onto India, and swirled around the Pacific. The carbon in the organic molecules of your cells was mined from the atmosphere by the plants that we eat. The salt in your sweat and tears, the calcium of your bones, and iron in your blood all eroded out of the rocks of Earth's crust; and the sulphur of the protein molecules in your hair and muscles was spewed out by volcanoes. The Earth has also provided us with the raw materials we have extracted, refined, and assembled into our tools and technologies, from the roughly fashioned hand-axes of the Stone Age, to today's computers and smart phones. These planetary influences drove our evolution in East Africa as a uniquely intelligent, communicative, and resourceful kind of creature. (Dartnell 2019, 1)

---

[1] Today, a vast range of literature exists on this cosmic horizon of our being and becoming. I recommend the following resources: Swimme and Berry (1992); Primark and Abrams (2007); Cannato (2010); Swimme and Tucker (2011); and Swimme (2022).

Note the concluding phrase of this quote: "a uniquely intelligent, communicative, and resourceful kind of creature." This perspective is so very different from inherited Christian notions of on original sin and our flawed condition. We are overtaken, not by a flawed deranged world, but by one in which everything is to be viewed and treated as gift. This is, indeed, countercultural, almost to the point of sheer exaggeration.

David Abram offers a valuable synthesis of the cosmic and planetary dimensions of our being and becoming:

> An eternity we thought was elsewhere now calls out to us from every cleft in every stone, from every cloud and clump of dirt. To lend our ears to the dripping glaciers—to come awake to the voices of silence—is to be turned inside out, discovering to our astonishment that the wholeness and holiness we've been drawing our way toward has been holding us all along; that the secret and sacred One that moves behind all the many traditions is none other than this animate immensity that enfolds us, this spherical eternity, glimpsed at last in its unfathomable wholeness and complexity, in its sensitivity and its sentience. (Abram 2010, 181)

Long before religion ever unfolded in the formal ways we know today, our ancient ancestors engaged with Holy Mystery and appropriated its benevolence through a range of rituals and ensuing ethical behaviors. A deep intuitive sense of the sacredness of creation itself, energized and sustained by the living Spirit—who blows with the wind, warms with fire heat, flows in the water, dances with the animals, and speaks in the vibrations of human sound—is central to this spiritual view.

Our Earthiness in Focus

Our affinity with the earth is encapsulated throughout our corporeal form as creatures of body-mind-spirit. Attending to our earthiness carries substantial weight for a new understanding of what it means to be human at both anthropological and religious levels. First, we must understand our evolutionary trajectory as God's timeline for our growth and development as an earth species. All the religions, and various ensuing theological theories, need to be realigned accordingly. Our foundational meaning as human beings is intimately wrapped up in our earthiness, and that interconnectedness has brought us to who and what we are today.

Second, we are not creatures with a superior way of being alive. Though we speak colloquially of a baby coming into the world, each of us is born out of the creative energy of the universe, channeled through the earth, and brought to fruition through the sexualized mediation of our parents. The aliveness that characterizes our existence has been given to us from the larger creation. Everything that constitutes our aliveness and enhances its advancement is given to us from the cosmic-earthly creation.

Third, receiving life itself as a gift of cosmic-earthly creation requires us to revisit the notion that we are ensouled beings and that our ensoulment separates us from and makes us superior to all other life-forms. Following on older Jain philosophy, Hinduism claims that the atman—breath or soul—is the universal, eternal self, of which each individual soul—jiva or jiva-atman—partakes. This seems to be the oldest evidence we have for the notion of soul.[2] As understood in Christianity, the soul is primarily a remnant of Greek philosophy, particularly from the influences of Plato and Aristotle at different periods in the development of Christian theology. It is a very recent development in the history of the human species and has now become a dangerously misleading concept. It should be replaced by the notion of Spirit-energy and an understanding of Jesus as a Spirit-filled person.

As earthlings with a seven-million-year story, we need to give discerning and devoted attention to our integration within our planetary home and our cosmic home. We belong to the earth,

---

[2] When anthropologists describe *animism*, they are not referring to soul, but rather to a spirit-energy that they suggest predates Axial Age religious belief.

God's Chosen Earthlings

and, with other creatures, we have roles to play as egalitarian co-operators rather than brutal competitors. When we attend to our relational embeddedness in the earth, we begin to pay more attention to the places in which we live each moment. Bioregionalism grounds us in deep connection with our earthly identity and can support us as we shed our religious arrogance and the strong patriarchal biases that often accompany it.

This earthly focus on human identity and meaning is slowly reentering the sphere of Christian spirituality and theology. Pope Francis's 2015 encyclical *Laudato Si'* is both original and revolutionary in its anthropological vision. "It cannot be emphasized enough how everything is interconnected. . . . It follows that the fragmentation of knowledge and the isolation of bits of information can actually become a form of ignorance, unless they are integrated into a broader vision of reality" (no. 138). Calling for an integral ecology, the encyclical challenges all people of good will to recognize that "nature cannot be regarded as something separate from ourselves or as a mere setting in which we live. We are part of nature, included in it and thus in constant interaction with it" (no. 139). Graced to be earthlings, we have a profound responsibility to live well with our fellow creatures.

Programmed to Cooperate

As a species we are endowed with an inherited capacity for cooperation. Many among us are not even aware of that fact. The fierce competition that is so endemic to our contemporary lifestyles leaves us with a deeply debilitating sense of woundedness. Our cultural ignorance toward cooperation is inherited, woven into the anthropology that I have presented in an earlier chapter. The capacity for cooperation is incarnationally inscribed in our very physiology:

> The cells themselves are cooperative organizations. Without extensive cooperation between the molecular processes and organelles that make up cells, we would not exist. Each of our million billion cells is made up

of thousands of incredibly small and intricate parts that cooperate together to produce the functions of the cell. We are cooperators that are made of cooperators, that are made of cooperators. It is cooperation all the way down. . . . Wherever evolution has been able to fully exploit the benefits of cooperation, we always find the extraordinary level of specialization and interdependency that results from a high degree of division of labor. We find it within cells, within our bodies, within our social systems, and between nations. And there is every reason to believe it will also be a feature of organizations that are capable of future evolutionary success on even larger scales. (Stewart 2000, 42, 45)

Our long human story is imbued with this relational orientation. The ethnological data from hunter-gatherer cultures are rich resources from which to surmise how Paleolithic hunter-gatherers structured their reality, living in bands consisting of fifteen to thirty people. Among our human ancestors, the hunter-gatherer band is the oldest known human social structure. There are still hunter-gatherer bands today, but precious few. Many of them are threatened with assimilation. However, hundreds of examples have been studied in the past century. Researchers have found that hunter-gatherers often live a life of economic, political, and social egalitarianism; all food and property shared. Anthropological research indicates that many times, at the band level, all members have the same political status; all are equal, and, it seems, there are no headmen or chiefs.

Political hierarchy doesn't come into play until society moves from bands to tribes to chiefdoms. In nomadic bands there is a natural prohibition on accumulation of material goods based on what you can carry. There is a decentralized system for distribution of goods, especially of meat. The band has built-in social devices that mitigate against bullying or selfishness. In *Hierarchy in the Forest: The Evolution of Egalitarian Behavior*, Christopher Boehm writes: "This egalitarian approach appears to be universal for foragers who live in small bands that remain nomadic, suggesting considerable antiquity for political egalitarianism." In Paleolithic times many of our most fundamental values in neoliberal capitalism, practices, such as ownership and private property, did not exist as we know it today. Kinship seems to have been predominantly matriarchal. Monotheism, with its sanctioning of the one supreme patriarchal authority, had not yet evolved.

"Hunter-gatherers almost everywhere are known for being fiercely egalitarian and going to great lengths to downplay competition and forestall ruptures in the social fabric, for reflexively shunning, humiliating, even ostracizing or executing those who behave in stingy, boastful, and antisocial ways," writes primatologist Sarah Blaffer Hrdy (Blaffer Hrdy 2009, 20). In fact, she goes so far as to claim that our propensity for cooperation precedes our acquisition of language, which is usually dated at 100,000 years ago (Blaffer Hrdy 2009, 38).

The human capacity for cooperation has been long ignored—and probably suppressed—as a valid field for exploration. In our time Matt Ridley launched a new wave of investigation in his 1996 publication *The Origins of Virtue*. The opening years of the twenty-first century have been marked by a plethora of new works, many of them rigorously scientific. These include the work of Sarah Blaffer Hrdy (2009); Jeremy Rifkin's acclaimed volume *The Empathic Civilization* (Rifkin 2010), highlighting the co-evolution of empathy and entropy in our time; Franz de Waal's *The Age of Empathy*, tracing our cooperative streak right back to some of our animal and primate ancestors (de Waal 2010); and Christopher Boehm's *Moral Origins* (2012), arguing that an ancient form of radical egalitarianism underpins our moral conscience; while Samuel Bowles and Herbert Gintis (2013) provide a scholarly genetic-based analysis of how cooperation and altruistic concern evolved in our species.

So what does all this mean today? We live in a world that has become saturated in the influence of mechanized artificial intelligence, with the growing prospect of intelligent machines taking over our lives and even outwitting our human intelligence. The technological entrepreneur Mustafa Suleyman provides a comprehensive overview of this contemporary evolutionary emergence, with its immense potential for promise and peril (Suleyman 2023). Consider the amount of time many of us already spend interconnecting through social and electronic media. This development is pushing our species into ever deeper realms of cooperation and collaboration. It is not negating what sustained us through much of our prehistoric existence but enhancing it and pushing its evolutionary potential to heights that are difficult to grasp or understand.

The Relational Matrix of Christianity

In *After Jesus Before Christianity: A Historical Exploration of the First Two Centuries of Jesus Movements*, Erin Vearncombe, Michael Peppard, and Hal Taussig (2022) closely reexamine what was transpiring within and around the Christian faith during the two centuries following the death and resurrection of Jesus. In broad strokes they review the archaeological, historical, and religious developments happening from the middle of the first century through to the beginning of the fourth century. As they highlight, these early Christian centuries were marked by a distinctive anti-imperial, postcolonial counterculture, a kind of people-power from the ground up that was facilitated through a range of small groups, associations, and anti-imperial networks. Although this egalitarian spirit was centered mainly on people and their desire to overthrow foreign colonization, it also embraced a range of ecological concerns. The long-held conviction that the land was God's primary gift to the people inspired several attempts to protect the land and reclaim it from the greed and usurpation of Roman land grabbing. Furthermore, they claim that this extensive and diverse sense of flexibility, variety, and creativity prevailed well into the 200s. The ecclesiastical conformity that has been emphasized in much of Christian history is a largely post-Constantine development that did not become normalized till the late 400s.

This view is supported by Peter Heather's work in church history. Heather claims that before Constantine's conversion, Christianity possessed no central authority (Heather 2022).

It was composed mainly of various urban congregations who elected their own leaders and, for the most part, ran their own affairs independently despite some commonalities in required beliefs, personal behavior, and institutional organization. Much remained in flux, and human ingenuity and creativity remained at the fore. This seems to be a very different perspective from the later ecclesial position on the flawed human condition!

What inspired this radical communitarian endeavor that became suppressed and even undermined by patriarchal church history? The central inspiration arises from a long-neglected prerogative of our gospel-based faith, usually translated as the kingdom of God, or more commonly today, the new reign of God. Dislocating and suppressing of this key concept seems to have been caused by the imperial understanding of divine kingship, which predates both Judaism and Christianity but was largely, if not totally, rejected by the historical Jesus.[3]

Here and in previous works I support the desire among a growing number of scripture scholars to move away from imperial language related to kings and kingdoms and, instead, use language that is likely to better represent what Jesus desired in the liberation and empowerment of gospel faith (O'Murchu 2017; 2021). To that end, I tend to use the Aramaic-related phrase *companionship of empowerment*. When it comes such renaming, I support John Dominic Crossan's encouragement to do our homework on what Jesus seems to have desired and adopt novel names in relevant language for our diverse cultural contexts in present Christian life and ministry (Crossan 2022).[4]

---

[3] Renowned Catholic scholar John P. Meier (d.2022) claims that the term *kingdom of God* is employed by Jesus in the gospel narratives in a way that has few if any precedents within Judaism or in any of the ancient religious sources predating Christianity (Meier 1994).

[4] "God's kingdom was to be the final fulfilment of biblical dreams for a world of distributive justice, the ideal realization of biblical hopes for a world of cosmic nonviolence, and the climax of biblical promises for a world of universal peace. . . . The specific phrase "Kingdom of God" is practically non-existent prior to Jesus' usage. So, a good translation should offer some hint as to why Jesus invented it as his own favourite designation for a transformed world and a transfigured earth" (Crossan 2022, 282).

The companionship of empowerment makes a double shift: from power-over to power-with, and from unilateral domination to communal collaboration (Crossan 2010). It marks a seismic shift from exclusivity to radical inclusiveness. As in our time, so also in the time of Jesus, the royal dispensation was heavily couched in elitism and exclusion. Royal patronage was often reserved to specific families. Even in the Roman imperial system, client-kings like Herod reigned in particular occupied areas. Within the exercise of kingly power, only the privileged few obtained close access. The king's palace was heavily fortified, and admission was only allowed to a selected elite. Opulence and glory befitted royal accolade, far in excess of what the ordinary people could ever hope to experience. A vast chasm stood between the king and the people.

Of the two key words, *companionship* is the more revolutionary, as it subtly denotes an all-important mutuality and community. Of course, *empowerment* could also be activated by a benevolent king. I contend, however, that Jesus would not be interested in any kind of king, benevolent or otherwise. He wanted an end to all forms of kingship, replacing them with a whole new empowering dynamic based on mutual participation and interdependence. He wanted every pyramid replaced with a circle and every hierarchy yielding pride of place to the holarchical structure that is evidenced throughout creation.[5] It seems that the historical Jesus declared an end to such imperial exclusion, a breakthrough captivated by Wendy Farley in these words: "In this empire (kingdom of God) neither victims nor perpetrators find the door slammed in their faces. . . . If we accept its healing, we are asked to accept that everyone else in the entire world is a citizen of this Kingdom" (Farley 2011, 204).

---

[5] Biologists frequently reference nested hierarchies that they detect throughout creation. I suspect that such observations arise from their academic conditioning, and thus they see what they expect to see—a kind of self-fulfilling prophesy favoring hierarchical structures rather than holarchical ones. For the holarchical understanding of creation, see Jude Currivan (2017).

In the companionship of empowerment, nobody is out. Everybody is included. Power and privilege are no longer reserved to the select few. The pyramid has been collapsed into a circle. Animation is activated from the center outward in an embrace that excludes no one. The "privileges" of this new dispensation belong primarily to those who have never known anything but exclusion: the poor, the marginalized, the despised, the disenfranchised. It has aptly been described as an upside-down kingdom (Kraybill 1990).

John Shelby Spong claims that Paul's extensive use of the notion of *righteousness*, frequently used in the letter to the Romans, may be considered an equivalent to the gospel notion of the kingdom of God, with the central focus on right relating in the name of love, justice, liberation, and empowerment:

> The kingdom of God comes when we are empowered to live fully, to love wastefully and to be all that we are capable of being. It means that the work of the kingdom of God is the work of enhancing human wholeness. . . . It means that the work of the kingdom of God is done when the eyes of the blind are opened to see reality undistorted by religious propaganda and the ears of the deaf are opened to listen to truth even when it threatens our religious security. It means that the limbs of the twisted, the crippled and the broken will be able to leap with joy as new humanity breaks in upon us without the distortions of our tribal past. It means that the voices of those once muted by fear can sing as they watch all the life-denying prejudices that separate human beings into destructive camps fade away and die. That will be the time when the kingdom of God becomes visible, and that will be when God's righteousness—for which, without always knowing it, human beings have both hungered and thirsted—will finally be revealed. (Spong 2016, 134, 140)

Thus far, I am emphasizing the significance of this new companionship for people, our relationship with God and with one another. It is cast in a radical new mode of inclusivity, empowerment, and liberation, and it resonates with the integrated earthly status described in the earlier part of this chapter. However, it seems that Jesus did not intend this new dispensation to be for humans only. He envisaged a call to discipleship that includes the entire creation, re-inviting humans to reclaim our long affiliation with the land and its inherent creative fertility.

Consider the insights of Elizabeth Johnson, Roger Haight, and Wes Howard-Brook, each recognizing a more inclusive good news in Jesus's mission:

> If separation is not the ideal, but connection is; if dualism is not the ideal but the relational embrace of diversity is; if hierarchy is not the ideal but mutuality is; then the kinship model more closely approximates reality. It sees human beings and the earth with all its creatures intrinsically related as companions in a community of life. Because we are all mutually interconnected, the flourishing or damaging of one ultimately affects all. (Johnson 1993, 30)[6]

> The rule of God refers to the intention of the Creator, the way God desires creation to be, especially human existence in a community that includes relationship with the wider life of the planet. . . . The rule of God represents no small insight. It symbolizes being drawn into the mystery of God's intention for the universe. . . . It opens up a framework of how human beings should live and what they should live for in this world. (Haight 2019, 214)

> Jesus of Nazareth proclaimed the "reign of God" in accordance with the pattern of the religion of creation,

---

[6] More recently, Elizabeth Johnson has written: "Since the reign of God is especially attentive to the needy and outcast, Jesus showed a partisanship for suffering people that we can today interpret as extending to encompass the earth and its myriads of distressed species and ecosystems. His ministry reveals a wideness in God's mercy that includes all creation" (Johnson 2018, 82).

while denouncing the religion of empire as a demonic counterfeit. (Howard-Brook 2016, xiii)

These three statements clearly assert that, for Jesus, the new companionship was not to be limited to humanity. Jesus's vision seems to be even less concerned with the preservation of human souls for a world hereafter. To the contrary, the new companionship embraces the entire cosmic and planetary creation, evoking a new horizon—or, perhaps, a very ancient one—in which an authentic human relationship with God is only possible as we relate more deeply with the creation we inhabit.[7]

Reworking the Theological Tradition

As a Christian practice, theology has long sought to protect and promote the primacy of God, the divine ruler of all creation. The notion of a ruling God is also part of many other major world religions, all of which evolved within the imperial aftermath of the Agricultural Revolution. Just as Jesus seems to have rejected this royal camouflage, turning it totally on its head, so, too, should all forms of formal religion revisit their notions of power and purge themselves of the deviant hunger for absolute power.

For contemporary Christians the foundational blueprint of our faith is stated unambiguously in the Sermon on the Mount: "But strive first for the kingdom of God and his righteousness, and all these things will be given to you as well" (Mt 6:33). Following Vearncombe, Peppard, and Moss, we can recognize how the faithful wrestled with this empowering and liberating vision for the first three hundred years of the Christian

---

[7] And it is not merely about being more inclusive of the wider web of life and how we are called to relate differently with all other earth creatures. According to Franciscan scholar Ilia Delio, it illuminates the mystery of the Godhead itself to a degree largely if not totally unknown in all previous attempts at an understanding of theodicy. Delio declares quite unambiguously: "Creation is not a backdrop for human drama but the disclosure of God's identity" (Delio 2011, 13). Divine identity and human identity are all of a piece within the interrelated web of creation.

narrative, before the paradigmatic shift under imperial favor. From the early fourth century this vision was suppressed and largely suffocated in the wake of Constantine's realignment of imperial traditions of Rome.

Today, Christians must reinstate the foundational inspiration of the companionship of empowerment for the sake of theological integrity, and we must honor and celebrate our paleoanthropological sacred inheritance as we do so. Apart from the archaeological evidence for the ritual burial of our dead, dating back some seventy thousand years, the creative legacy that we have explored here evidences an incarnational presence of our God going back into deep time.

The incarnation of our God in the life and ministry of the historical Jesus did not begin with Jesus of Nazareth. It began seven million years ago in East Africa as our creative God became embodied anew in the newly evolving earthling *Sahelanthropus tchadensis*. And at every stage of our evolutionary growth that same God has been present with and to us, primarily recognized in the energizing presence of the Great Spirit. The incarnational God, who became an embodied presence in and with us across this grand evolutionary narrative, was not looking ahead on a timeline, anticipating the redeeming liberation offered through the historical Jesus. Rather, in the coming of the historical Jesus, God affirms, confirms, and celebrates all we achieved throughout our evolutionary story because we seem to have gotten it right most of the time. Yes, we got it right, because we remained very close to nature, integrating our God-given identity as earthlings well.

Any theology today that is unable to embrace this enlarged horizon will fail to liberate or empower either humans or the earth we inhabit. Such a theology will also fail to liberate our Christian inheritance from the shackles of imperial contagion. Healthy theology must empower us to reclaim what we should never have compromised or betrayed in the first place: the new reign of God—the companionship of empowerment—the light that illuminates the creativity of our God at work in every sphere of creation.

4

The Grace of Human Creativity

We are projects of collective self-creation. What if we approached human history that way? What if we treat people from the beginning as imaginative, intelligent, playful creatures who deserve to be understood as such?
—DAVID GRAEBER AND DAVID WENGROW

I saw an angel in the marble and carved until I set him free.
—MICHELANGELO

Human depravity is widely presumed to have been the default position of our species throughout much of its evolutionary history. In this largely unquestioned assumption, we tend to be described as primitive, ignorant, barbaric, and driven by raw instinct. It is also assumed that we survive through brutality and violence, the survival of the fittest!

This powerful contagion, let loose in and through our species, affects the entire creation. Religious traditions have even argued that, because we got it wrong in some mythic past, everything has been tainted at best. Of course, the underlying assumption here is that humans are a class apart, superior to every other life-form on the planet. When we get it wrong, then everything malfunctions throughout the entire web of life. Some religionists go along with this rather negative view of life, as if it has always been that way and there is not a great deal we can do about it. We must be rescued, they surmise, by a distant, redeeming God. In this story God saves us from the plight of our own destiny. Through an evolutionary lens, these claims are a very recent, deluded set of suppositions that have emerged and been developed over the last few thousand years.

The Patriarchal Context

When, where, and how did the myth of flawed humanity come into being? Many of the myths of human origins, and particularly the Christian and Jewish stories in Genesis, postulate an original state of harmony and wholeness that came to an end when we fell from grace. The creation stories in Genesis are more recent than the myths of human origins in some of the other religious traditions. Other, older myths of human origins begin to appear in the record some four thousand years ago. Hinduism emerged through this fertile religious milieu in the Indus River Valley, incorporating many different religious traditions. In Egypt, early monotheism begins to form with the cult of Aten in the 1300s BCE. Judaism itself coalesces into something we might recognize today during the Hebrew exile in Babylon in the 500s BCE. Many myths of origin in this epoch begin with deities entering and affecting creation, using humans to carry forward their desires and plans for creation. In most cases humans fail to fulfill the wishes of the gods.

Many of the gods are described as superior beings from another realm, with kinglike power, domination, and control. In these stories we encounter a great deal of human imagination, projecting an ancient imperial consciousness. The sociopolitical evolution of monarchies and "the king" is recent in our human story. Lieven has argued convincingly that they emerged about six thousand years ago (Lieven 2022). Part of this evolution was a theological claim that the king is derived from the divine god-king who rules from above the sky. The movement toward the imperial rule of kings arose through previous cultures of domination, associated with the Agricultural Revolution. Though humans had been cultivating land and gathering from the fertility of land and soil for thousands of years, major cultural adjustments arose through drastic climate changes, including severe freezing, about twelve thousand years ago (see Graeber and Wengrow 2021, 500).[1]

As is happening today, drastic climate changes created a culture of panic and extensive dislocation. Where they could, humans became much more settled and sedentary in attempts to control variables in their food supply through cultivation. The land became a resource to produce livestock and food crops instead of a living, breathing entity. These processes led to the parceling out of land among competing parties, encouraging people to become ever more demanding and competitive in early marketplaces. Enclosure of lands led to the establishment and violent enforcement of geographic territory claims. In the modern period the nation-state would emerge as the sovereign to replace the monarch, claiming the exclusive right to use violence to enforce its claims over a population.

All of this was made possible through a new, arrogant subgroup that was determined to master the vagaries of nature, according to Genesis, making man the master of creation. Today, this has been called the patriarchal system, morphing through kings and kingdoms, validated and affirmed in the name of a ruling God. It is God who is the primary patriarch of all that exists. Alongside these sociopolitical developments, Classical Greek philosophical anthropology prioritized human autonomy and rationality as the keys to our exceptionality. Imbued with a rational soul, man was next to God as governor of an irrational and violent world. As Christian theology adopted and sanctioned—literally, made holy—this philosophical anthropology positioned humans as rational functionaries, assisting the ruling God in mastering a wayward creation. As we moved through Late Antiquity and the Middle Ages, into Modernity, only humans of the recent millennia were thought

---

[1] Usually associated with an icecap spreading down over what today we know as mainland Europe. However, I tend to favor an alternative view propounded by British scholar Steve Taylor (2005), who claims that the major impact of the ice age was on what is now the Sahara of North Africa and present-day Saudi Arabia, creating the desertification we know up to the present time.

capable of being God's chosen helpers. Humans of earlier times were nothing more than primitive pagans, of no value to God or creation.

Reclaiming Our Authentic Story

This perverse, degrading human narrative lingers with us, albeit in modified forms. Unfortunately, much of the human violence and exploitation that characterizes our world today gives credence for such a view. In our so-called civilized world, we evidence an overwhelming sense of oppression and barbarity. Unreflectively, a lot of people conclude that, if we are this bad, then our ancestors must have been much worse. A myth of progress is on full display. This conclusion is precisely the outcome that ensues when we fail to honor our full human evolutionary story. For much, if not all, of our long evolutionary story, we behaved in constructive, creative ways, precisely because we remained very close to nature, thus honoring our identity as earthlings.

The growing body of data gathered from the hunter-gatherer stage of our existence indicates that, at least as far back as two million years ago, our ancestors lived in small, mobile groups, probably not exceeding fifty persons, and survived on a subsistence lifestyle based on hunting and food gathering. With the onset of the Agricultural Revolution, that lifestyle came to an end for many humans. Drawing largely on the pioneering work of the British anthropologist James Woodburn, Graeber and Wengrow describe this alternative overview of the hunter-gatherer culture prior to the onset of the Agricultural Revolution:

> In all parts of the world, small communities formed civilizations in that true sense of extended moral communities. Without permanent kings, bureaucrats or standing armies they fostered the growth of mathematical and calendric knowledge. In some regions they pioneered metallurgy, the cultivation of olives, vines and date palms, or the invention of leavened bread and wheat beer; in others,

they domesticated maize and learned to extract poisons, medicines, and mind-altering substances from plants. Civilizations, in the true sense, developed the major textile technologies applied to fabrics and basketry, the potter's wheel, stone industries and beadwork, the sail and maritime navigations. A moment's reflection shows that women, their work, their concerns and innovations, are at the core of this more accurate understanding of civilization. (Graeber and Wengrow 2021, 433)

This description fits well for the millennia immediately preceding the Agricultural Revolution, perhaps back to about 20,000 BCE. However, the sense of egalitarianism noted by James Woodburn (1982), Christopher Boehm (2012), and Agustin Fuentes (2017) belongs to a much earlier phase of our evolution as a human species. Our ancient human story surfaces potentialities for human creativity and innovation that defy and undermine the negative anthropology of more recent times.[2]

Our Ancient Artistic Flair

Our prehistoric sense of creativity tends to be traced back to the time of Ice Age Art, usually dated between forty thousand and fifteen thousand years ago. Scholars are beginning to look to much older evidence related to toolmaking, a historical development focused on practical usefulness with an articulation of the human urge to become ever more creative as we engage life and our inhabited world. Kathy Schick and Nicholas Toth (1994) are among today's pioneering researchers of this ancient creativity. In 2003, they founded the Stone Age Institute, a nonprofit education and research facility dedicated to research into human origins, where they are co-directors and executive board members. They have conducted archaeo-

---

[2] This is not merely an attempt to retrieve the noble savage, associated with the work of French philosopher René Rousseau. We are dealing with something far more complex and profound.

logical field research and studied the lithic assemblages from Oldowan and Acheulean sites, including the Olduvai Gorge in Tanzania, Koobi Fora in Kenya, Damanisi in Georgia, Gona and Middle Awash in Ethiopia, Nihewan Basin in China, and Ambrona in Spain.

In 2014, in collaboration with other researchers, they began the Olduvai Gorge Coring Project, extracting geological cores around the gorge in order to increase our knowledge of the geological history of the Olduvai Gorge area and surface more reliable evidence for ancient human stone technology. Their primary focus now is cognitive archaeology, attempting to assess the levels of intelligence, problem-solving abilities, and symbolic behavior of past hominins by examining the patterns that can be gleaned from the archaeological record through evolutionary time.

The Oldowan Industrial Complex is one of the better known archaeological sites that shows a range of stone technologies that date back to at least 2.6–2.5 million years ago. These technologies tend to be characterized by simple core forms made on cobbles or chunks. They also include a range of flakes that require even more sophisticated cognitive, creative, and practical skills. From material like this, David Frayer has concluded that the brain lateralization of *Homo habilis* was more like that of modern *Homo sapiens* than that of other apes (Frayer 2016). Frayer found striations on the teeth of a 1.8-million-year-old *Homo habilis* fossil that indicate a skillful right-handedness. It also seems that *Homo habilis* could encode perceptions of events in memory and recall them in the presence of a cue. Excavations at the Ethiopian site of Gona provide evidence that Oldowan hominins preferentially selected higher-quality materials from rock sources. These early toolmakers were able to identify and preferentially select higher quality materials like finer-grained volcanic materials with fewer phenocrysts, which could produce hard, sharp edges when flaked. Research has highlighted the high quality of the trachyte raw material that Oldowan toolmakers selected as indicative of a capacity for perceptual discrimination long thought to have been impossible for such ancient peoples. Anne Delagnes and Helene Roche, using an approach known as *chaîne opératoire*, identified how the toolmakers had a well-developed mastery of knapping skills and techniques in a study at the 2.34-million-year-old site of Lokalalei 2C (Delagnes and Roche 2005). Moreover, they argued that the overall lithic assemblage shows planning and foresight in the choices and use of raw materials.

Imagination, Visualization, Discrimination

The origin and increasing sophistication of toolmaking reveals an increasingly complex sense of symmetry, which is a function of the visual brain. The tools named as the Oldowan and Acheulian types represent a period of some two million years, during which time the brain of our hominin ancestors expanded and tools became more advanced. In studies using brain-scanning technology, researchers have observed brain activation during toolmaking that includes both visuomotor and language circuits. This suggests that toolmaking and language share a basis in the human capacity for complex, goal-directed manual activity.[3] In these connections we are encountering artistic creativity through evidence of the increasing sophistication of tool technology and of increasing brain size. Together, these data suggest that our ancient ancestors had the ability to create art or proto-art much earlier in evolution than is suggested by current knowledge of art-related artifacts. Human perceptions of visual imagination and discrimination arise within our brains and can range from alternative perceptions of simple objects and drawings to higher levels of imagination, such as the interpretation of facial expression in a painting. This is not just about our early ancestors seeing their own human likeness in something like a stone. This is about a symbolic response arising from the creative imagination.

---

[3] This is a highly controversial claim as most scholars date the evolution of language to about 100,000 years ago, and most still hold the view that the human capacities for imagination, intuition, and creative visualization could not have existed before humans learned to speak. For an alternative point of view, see Deacon (1997).

Gowlett has discussed the necessity of the Acheulian toolmaker to see the outline of the tool in the mind's eye or to use a "visuospatial sketchpad" (Gowlett 1984). The creation of an Acheulian biface—a hand-axe worked on both sides—by *Homo erectus* in East Africa involved, first, the choice of a stone with a correctly curved surface. A series of actions that followed a defined set of instructions then occurred. These instructions are a virtual manual, memorized by demonstration and repetition. The instructions involved the formation of separate planes along different axes, minimizing the computational complexities required to create the three-dimensional finished product. Some skill and intelligence at work here!

In 2010, a startling announcement was made. Two bones with stone-tool butchery marks dated at 3.39 million years ago had been found at the Dikika site in Ethiopia, pushing back the earliest traces of stone-tool-assisted eating of hoofed animals to approximately eight-hundred-thousand years earlier than previously known (McPherron et al. 2010). This was also far earlier than the earliest *Homo* fossils. Researchers have concluded that *Australopithecus afarensis* used stone tools to assist their eating of hoofed animals. Could it be that we are also witnessing something of a more sophisticated, imaginative set of skills with possible artistic intent earlier than we have imagined?

Scientific research continues to delve deeper for possible creative breakthroughs. In May 2015, the discovery of 3.3-million-year-old stone tools from the Lomekwi 3 site in Kenya was announced, pushing back the origin of stone toolmaking by 700,000 years. Just two months earlier, in March 2015, a 2.8-million-year-old fossil mandible and teeth from the Ledi-Geraru research area in Ethiopia were uncovered. The jaw predates the previously known fossils of the *Homo* lineage by approximately 400,000 years. These fossils have not been assigned to a particular species of early *Homo*, but it is now accepted that they are the earliest fossils of our genus.

Dietrich Stout has worked to replicate the stone-technology behavior of our ancient ancestors. Stout has set up a pioneering project, working collaboratively with a team of neuroscientists, to detect brain activity during prolonged sessions of stone knapping (Stout 2016). Consistently, the brain activity being recorded and observed in these sessions evidences high levels of creativity, supporting the notion of what Colin Renfrew calls "the sapient mind" (Renfrew 2009). Recently, AI entrepreneur Mustafa Suleyman has written, "Technology has a clear, inevitable trajectory: mass diffusion in great roiling waves. This is true from the earliest flint and bone tools to the latest AI models" (Suleyman 2023, 25). Here, technology is no mere mechanical prowess, nor is it pursued to control an otherwise alien environment. It arises from a deep inner creativity, subconsciously imbued with purpose and meaning. This same drive for meaning underlies the pursuit of AI in our time.

The Artistic Flair

A growing body of evidence for ancient creativity marks this new departure for our understanding of human nature. "We tend to think of these beautiful cave paintings of the big mastodons and wild oryx as art. But that's only about 40,000 years old," Agustin Fuentes notes. There is a long-held view that modern human behavior, including art, only began when *Homo sapiens* migrated from Africa to Europe around forty-five thousand years ago. "We know that 85,000 years ago, in southern Africa, our ancestors were carving on ostrich eggshells. Twenty thousand years earlier than that," Fuentes continues, "they were drilling holes in small shells and wearing them around their necks." As we could come to terms with the sixty-thousand-year-old-creativity that is evidenced in what is known as Ice Age Art, now discovered in Europe, Africa, Indonesia, we open up other possibilities for a more accurate and authentic understanding of human nature that reaches even farther back. Fuentes concludes:

> One hundred thousand years before [we drilling those holes and wearing worked shells], they were crumbling ochre and rubbing it on their bodies. Five hundred thousand years

before that, half a million years ago, they were making tools that were incredibly beautiful and more symmetrical and aesthetic than they had to be to do their jobs. Art is very deep in human history. (quoted in Worrall 2017)

The human love of body decoration also involves several creative dimensions. Modern cosmetics and tattoos have a long history, probably originating with the use of ochre for coloring the skin hundreds of millennia ago. The oldest known use of ochre is about 164,000 BCE from a South African coastal site, Pinnacle Point, where fifty-seven pigment pieces were found. At least ten of the pieces had been ground or scraped. These had been deliberately selected as the most intensely red pigments. The possibility that they were used for body coloring has been accepted on the basis of this color selection, as none of the other possible functions of ochre would require this. Body decoration, whether with pigments or with beads made from pierced shells such as those found in the Blombos caves of South Africa—dated to about 100,000 BCE—suggests highly developed cognitive functions and extensive exploration of symbolic meaning (Henshilwood 2009).

This pioneering endeavor challenges and even undermines the long-held view among language researchers that human creativity through intelligence, imagination, and intuition was only possible after language evolved, approximately 100,000 years ago. It has long been assumed that, prior to that time, humans were no better than animals in our ability to perceive and comprehend. Only after language have the ingredients of human intelligence fallen into place, or so we have been told. Humans, in this story, slowly evolved the capacity to engage their environment in more intelligently informed ways after language came on the scene. This view could be described as *the restrictive language hypothesis*.

Kenneth Oakley's argument that our ancient toolmakers were endowed with an intelligent and even artistic flair renders the restrictive language hypothesis indefensible. As neuro-anthropologist Terence Deacon indicates, language does not mark the beginning of more advanced human intelligibility, incorporating human creativity and a capacity for symbolism (Deacon 1997). Rather, language is the outcome of a species that has been portraying such creativity over several thousand years, co-creating the critical evolutionary threshold that leads to language as we understand it today.

To date, the oldest evidence for our human artistic flair tends to be traced to Lower Paleolithic times. Two discoveries are frequently cited: the Venus of Berekhat Ram (c.230,000–700,000 BCE) and the Venus of Tan-Tan (c.300,000–500,000 BCE). These are generally considered to be the products of *Homo neanderthalensis*. Most scholars consider the oldest known art in the world to be the Bhimbetka Petroglyphs, ten cupules and a groove, discovered in the quartzite auditorium rock shelter at Bhimbetka in Madhya Pradesh, central India, dating to at least 290,000 BCE.

Human creativity is much older and more insinuated into our evolutionary flourishing than we have ever suspected. This is the long-repressed truth that we need to reclaim in an anthropological narrative that must overcome the primitive assumptions to which science and religion have been wedded for far too long. Fortunately, more rigorous science invites us to such daring new horizons. Christopher Collins explores the cognitive skills that predate language and writing, including the brain's capacity to perceive the visible world, store its images, and retrieve them later to form simulated mental events (Collins 2013). Long before hominins could share stories through speech, they perceived, remembered, and imagined their world in a range of pre-verbal narratives.

We can no longer assume that the earliest stone technology served merely a functional endeavor with rational and pragmatic purposes. Although we have no concrete evidence for an artistic dimension to date, Dietrich Stout's research requires us to keep open the possibility—even the likelihood—that such evidence will be forthcoming. In our species and our heritage the capacity for creativity seems considerably older than we currently assume.

System theorist Jeremy Lent supports these same conclusions. He draws on evidence from the social sciences to claim that a patterning instinct pervades the entire creation, influencing human perception and understanding even in the realm of deep time:

> Our patterning instinct honed over millions of years to find meaning in the complex experience of daily life, plays a crucial role in the drive to imbue our own mental characteristics into the world around us. In prelinguistic times, its powers helped early humans successfully navigate their increasingly sophisticated communities. With the emergence of language, it drove infants to impute meaning into the cacophony of sounds with which they were bombarded. With its unrelenting compulsion for patterning, its prowess was then applied to look for meaning in the otherwise seemingly chaotic occurrences of the universe. (Lent 2017, 76)[4]

The Religious Dimension

As already noted, the formal religions we know today are very recent visitors to our human world. Religious traditions have developed "Golden Rules" of love and compassion. They have empowered people to deal with pain and calamity, as well. They have also reinforced the imperial consciousness of the post-Agricultural era. By evolving narrow anthropologies that are preoccupied with the salvation of the human soul, some have even given humans a beneficial status above and beyond every other creature in creation. Religious traditions have been forces for domination and oppression, examples of which are still visible in the contemporary world.[5]

---

[4] Beyond the human level we note that German mathematician Emmy Noether (1882–1935) highlighted a patterning process throughout creation, a claim that mainline science only formally recognized in the latter half of the twentieth century (for more, see Clegg 2021).

[5] Examples that spring to mind include the Taliban's enforcement of Islamic law, the endorsement of violence by some Buddhists in both Sri Lanka and Myanmar, and the marginalization of women in several Christian fundamentalist groups.

Prior to the Agricultural Revolution, spirituality flourished in a range of forms. The caves associated with Ice Age Art were probably sites devoted to a complex range of religious and spiritual behaviors. There is still considerable debate on how we interpret this art. Some claim that we should simply view it as art for art's sake. Some still adhere to the opinion of archaeologist and anthropologist Henri Brueil, who viewed it as a form of sympathetic magic related to hunting in particular. Claude Lévi-Strauss, representing a structuralist interpretative tradition, argued that the painted animal images are best interpreted as mythic totems. Andre Leroi-Gorham, with a particular interest in the Lascaux site, drew up an inventory of the various images being employed and did not discern any overall meaning. Finally, Jean Clottes and David Lewis Williams (1998) have favored shamanistic interpretations in which the art possibly contributed to trance states, dancing, drumming, and fasting. Their position indicates a strong spiritual motif and a highly creative approach to ritual, worship, and devotion.[6]

Representations of a human body with an animal head, suggesting shamanic motifs, are among the cave-art images. Some Upper Paleolithic figures, known as therianthropes, are believed to be inspired from shamanic practices. A lion-headed man carved in mammoth ivory is one of the best known of these figures. It has been dated to 30,000–34,000 BCE, and it is from southwest Germany. The oldest known example of a therianthropic figure was painted on rock in the same date range—32,000–34,000 BCE—in red ochre. That figure represents a man with either an animal head or horned headdress and was found in Fumane Cave in Italy. The Upper Paleolithic examples of therianthropes in French caves—Volp, Ariège, Gabaillou, and Lascaux—have one important factor in common: they are all in the deepest, most inaccessible parts of the cave, where no natural light penetrates. Although the most common interpretation of these composite figures is that they represent

---

[6] A great deal of research on Ice Age Art continues, with the following among the valuable informed resources: Paul Bahn (1997), Jill Cook (2013), David Lewis-Williams (2002), and Ofer Bar-Yosef (2002).

shamans of a kind, an alternative or additional possibility is that they represent a god who was master of animals (Clottes and Lewis-Williams 1998).

The religious beliefs of contemporary tribal peoples, particularly their notion of the Great Spirit, may throw light on the kind of spirituality adopted by our ancestors over several thousands of years. In the case of Ice Age Art, symbolic contact with the spirit world can be made by placing the hands on the wall. Negative or stenciled hand prints, produced by placing a hand on the wall and blowing pigment around it and between the fingers, are found throughout world rock art, in European caves and on rocks from Australia, America, and South Africa (Clottes 2008). In the scholarly literature this attribution of the sacred is often described as *animism*, a concept often traced to British anthropologist Edward B. Tylor.[7] Tylor claims that the ancient peoples saw something like a soul in animals, trees, and other objects in the natural world. But this attribution is not helpful, as the notion of the soul that Tylor uses is of very recent origin, largely developed by Plato and Aristotle. We are on much more reliable ground when we attribute such religious sentiment to that of spirit-power, the approach adopted by more recent analysts such as Nurit Bird-David (1999), Stewart Guthrie (2000), or Graham Harvey (2006). That sense of living spirit that energizes all things in creation, sustaining humans themselves in that interconnected web of life, is a form of human consciousness that we have imbibed and lived for several thousand years. That same spirit-centered pervasive sacredness might have underpinned ancient rituals like the burial of our dead, adopted by *Homo neanderthalensis* at least seventy-thousand years ago.

While comparisons with contemporary Indigenous Peoples must not be made too easily or literally, their extensive beliefs in pervasive spirit-power, known by some as the Great Spirit,

---

[7] His classic work on the subject is *Primitive Culture: Researches into the Development of Mythology, Philosophy, Religion, Art, and Custom*, published in 1871.

might well provide valuable information on the animism of ancient times. When Indigenous/First Nations Peoples adopt the notion of the Great Spirit, they are not referring to some transcendent divine being outside the world, but neither are they describing a pantheistic deity empowering creation from within. Instead, they are asserting the potential of the land and the soil to awaken a sense of sacredness through the ever-intricate dimensions of earth life, to reveal complexity, creativity, and meaning. In this approach the earth is alive with a quality of aliveness that supersedes that of our human way of being alive. Everything in our embodied existence is given to us from the larger web of life. In that gifted endowment, we are energized by that which empowers all creation, that life force which Christian theology names as the Holy Spirit of God. In our close affiliation with that alive earth, we intuitively connect with this spirit-power. We have been articulating the connection through a range of ritual behaviors for thousands, if not millions, of years before religions or churches ever came to be.

Rightly, then, recent movements for recognizing personhood throughout creation have gained momentum. The New Zealand government, in 2017, responded to decades of Māori activism and declared the Whanganui River to be a legal person, a gesture that might well be described as animism taking a legal form. Or, perhaps, it may more accurately be described as declaring the river itself to be an abode of living spirit, meriting the reverence and respect we attribute to all sentient beings.

Where Grace Abounds

St. Paul, in his various letters, seems to be keenly aware of the sinfulness of the human condition and its deleterious effects on the world generally. Yet, for Paul, sin is not the dominant force (Rom 5:20). Grace abounds all the more! Such grace is a free gift released into the world through the death and resurrection of Jesus. Had Paul been aware of the ancient creativity highlighted in this chapter, perhaps he might have cited it as evidence for his claim that grace, not sin, is the primary reality of our human condition.

Unfortunately, scholars have also extracted pieces of Paul's letter to the Roman Christians to support their logic of original sin (Rom 5:12–21). Here, Paul draws on the Genesis story of the Garden of Eden, framing it within the Jesus narrative. Christian theories of original sin began to emerge in the third century and only became fully formed with the writings of Augustine of Hippo (354–430 AD). Influenced by Augustine, the Council of Carthage (411–18 AD) and the Council of Orange (529 AD) set in motion the theological speculations that eventually led to what continues to be an official teaching of many Christian churches.

The doctrine of original sin depends on a narrative of original perfection. Learning from our evolutionary story, however, we recognize that there has never been an original perfection, so there could never have been a fall from perfection to call original sin. As an evolving species woven through an evolving cosmos, ours is a story of mixed fortunes, getting it beautifully right sometimes and drastically wrong at other times. Therein lies the price we pay for our freedom and creativity. However, the more we delve deeply into our long story, the more we fail to find evidence for persistent wrongdoing and sinfulness. We seem to be get it right most of the time, precisely when we remain very close to nature.

Several years ago Matthew Fox expressed it very well in his claim that we are first and foremost beneficiaries of an original blessing, not victims of an original sin (Fox 1983). If our politics, economics, and churches had followed that guideline, there is good reason to believe that we would be dealing very differently with our world today, honoring the more foundational orientation of the wisdom and creativity that are so endemic to our growth and development as an evolutionary species.

5

God beyond the Culture of Civilization

What then surely is most new about our modern understanding of life is the idea of evolution, for it enables us to see life not as an eternally repeating cycle, but as a process that continually generates and discovers novelty.

—Lee Smolin

Christianity is not a new religion but the end of tribal religion, evoking a new type of person for a new type of world.

—Ilia Delio

In his oft-cited work *Primitive Culture* (1871), Edward Burnett Tylor argues for a type of cultural evolution involving three specific stages of cultural development: savagery, barbarism, and civilization. The first encompasses cultures based on hunting and gathering. The second describes cultures based on nomadic herding and agriculture. The third includes cultures based on writing and the urban lifestyle, evolving around 3,000 BCE. Tylor was also one of the first anthropologists to use the term *animism* to describe the ancient religious belief in a world inhabited by spirit-forces, both benign and evil.[1]

---

[1] South African anthropologist Adam Kuper (2017) provides a valuable overview and critique of how the notion of the primitive came to be used in anthropology (and other related studies), along with a contemporary critique of its negative and superficial connotations.

"Primitive society" functioned as a label for some form of social organization that, for long, kept us locked into an arrested form of development. Regardless of factual accuracy, the label aimed to emphasize the value of our current relationship paradigm, "civilization." According to these early anthropologists, "primitive society" was left behind as we evolved into a civilized people.

This view has had some formidable champions, among them Auguste Comte, Sir James George Frazer, Lucien Lévy-Bruhl, and G. W. F. Hegel. One of the first anthropologists to challenge the prevailing ideology and support an alternative viewpoint was Claude Lévi-Strauss. In his many works, particularly his 1966 *The Savage Mind*, Lévi-Strauss argued that this interpretation of the primitive is factually and theoretically indefensible. He asserted that the primitive was not a "savage" who was governed only by his bodily impulses and who thought, if at all, in merely utilitarian terms. Lévi-Strauss emphasized that the "primitive" people were capable of discerning organic interconnectedness with the wider web of life. Their desires were not limited merely to those things that are "good to eat" but extended to a relational embrace and integration of surrounding ecological niches. In more recent times scholars from a range of different disciplines have suggested that the closeness to the natural world and integration with it as earthlings enabled unique, organic relationships for prehistoric humans, both among themselves and with the several other life-forms that constituted the world of their experience.

Their ancient integration carried religious and spiritual significance. The openness of ancient cultures to the world of natural forms may have allowed them to experience the world as a sacred reality, in a mode of revelation called a hierophany. Notably, such experiences cannot be reduced to the rational, the irrational, or the psychological. Integrating many seemingly disparate and often opposed experiences into a unified vision is part of how religious symbols can help us humans understand our world.

Toward a Discerning Mind and Heart

In recent years, especially among anthropologists, we have become much more sensitive and discerning about inherited wisdom from the past, cherishing what might still be relevant for the present and future while highlighting derogatory understandings of the past that need to be discarded and consigned to historical archives. With that emerging awareness, we now stand a better chance of engaging a genuine discernment on the sacred creativity that characterizes our long evolutionary story. Meanwhile, there remains what postcolonial scholars call the *residue*, cultural constructs that are still prevalent but no longer serve us well as we seek to create a more integrated spirituality for the twenty-first century. The notion of a civilized way of doing things is central to such constructs. Here, civilization is envisaged in the aftermath of the Agricultural Revolution.

Creatures of Imperial Power

Were humans always hungry for power and control? Those of a Darwinian evolutionary persuasion might respond affirmatively, asserting that such a desire is essential to evolutionary progress. The mechanism that Darwin proposed for evolution is natural selection. Because resources are limited in nature, organisms with heritable traits that favor survival and reproduction will tend to leave more offspring than their peers, causing the traits to increase in frequency over generations. This process has been misinterpreted as a two-tier system of the strong and the weak, favoring the strong and the mighty over the more vulnerable. Interpreting Darwin this way is very much an anthropocentric approach that does not make sense in a broader evolutionary creation that is characterized by processes of creation through destruction and interdependent ecological living.

Not all scholars accept this power-based interpretation. Jeremy Rifkin asks,

> Is it possible that human beings are not inherently evil or intrinsically self-interested and materialistic, but are of a very different nature—an empathic one—and that all of the other drives that we have considered to be primary—aggression, violence, selfish behaviour, acquisitiveness—are in fact secondary drives that flow from the repression or denial of our most basic instinct? (Rifkin 2010, 18)

Bishop John Shelby Spong has written:

> Atonement theology assumes that we were created in some kind of original perfection. We now know that life has emerged from a single cell that evolved into self-conscious complexity over billions of years. *There was no original perfection*, so there could never have been a fall from perfection. . . . What human life needs is not a theology of human degradation. That is what atonement theology gives us. What we need is a theology of human fulfilment. (Spong 2016, 203, 209)

A theology of human fulfillment seems to integrate the spirit of Rifkin's question within the theological concerns that we have identified earlier. A theology of human fulfillment calls us to recognize that and how we humans are at home as earthlings in the household of creation. We have, throughout our history, been good relatives with our kindred creation when we remained very close to nature. When we have not been good, life-affirming relatives, we are called back and into more convivial, nonviolent ways of relating and behaving. The crucial issue in a theology of human fulfillment is not power-as-domination but mutual empowerment that emerges through more egalitarian and interconnected ways of being.

Creatures of Rational Discourse

For Classical Greeks, only those endowed with the faculty of rational thought and discourse could hope to govern. The rational simultaneously advanced their own power and mistakenly assumed that their special rule would advance other life-forms. According to Greek philosophers, particularly Plato and Aristotle, only males are fully equipped with the power of reason. Women's life experiences are so enmeshed in emotion and hysteria that they are largely, if not totally, unable to rise to such a challenge. As for the rest of the created universe, only humans possess a rational soul—in Aristotle. This uniqueness entitles them to be lords over everything else in creation.

Societies that have emerged from and valued the intellectual contributions of the Classical Greeks—societies like our own Euro-American neoliberal one—have tangled power, rationality, and sometimes religious fervor in destructive ways. Together, anthropocentric imperialism and excessive rationality condition humans to perceive ourselves as the end of the evolutionary line in terms of intelligent beings instead of the progeny of an evolutionary process. Scientists and theologians alike have contributed to the "Empire of Reason," producing tremendous technological marvels. These technological advances and the processes of thought behind them are haunting our world as never before. This old paradigm is disintegrating in the face of planetary destruction. The consequences of their own destructive acts terrify the powers that be.

Intriguingly, anthropological explorations of our human past can help us move through this disintegrating paradigm and experience healthy relationality as earthlings anew. If the power-as-domination and prioritization of rational power are recent anthropological convictions, what preceded them? What did our ancient ancestors consider to be the life-principle of the body? Anthropological notions of animism may offer valuable insights, with the information we now possess on ancient artwork being significantly relevant. Our ancient ancestors experienced the presence and influence of an animating energy for which the notion of *spirit* is far more appropriate than that of a rational soul that wills to dominate.

Religion as a Mechanism for Management and Control

Theologians and scholars of religion have gone to great lengths to highlight the positive, life-enhancing qualities of religious belief and practice. Tenets and practices of different religious traditions that contribute to well-being are held up in multi-faith settings as sites for common ground, for positive relationships, and for healthy life together amid difference. While I support positive appraisals of religious life, I also think that we cannot ignore or underestimate features of religious traditions that are oppressive and destructive. We live in a complex world, and our evaluation of religious and spiritual traditions must attend to this complexity.

Especially in cases of those that have emerged through shadows of patriarchal cultures, religious cultures and cults have contributed significantly to sociopolitical control of and domination over people and land. Hierarchical systems within religious traditions, particularly when coupled with imperial political aspirations and authorities, have been established and supported in different ways across different cultures. In Catholicism, for instance, the magisterium has served as an institution for this control mechanism through the Congregation (now Dicastery) for the Doctrine of the Faith. Hierarchical systems, however complex, ultimately depend on a binary division between those who rule—often claiming a divine mandate—and those who obey. In Christian traditions unquestioned obedience to the earthly representatives of God has led to an anthropocentric entanglement that has completely overlooked the sacredness of creation. Instead of enhancing our earthly life, righteous obedience in this tradition only values the experience of an afterlife in some other plane of existence.

In multi-faith settings internal religious hierarchies can emphasize each religion's claims to absolute uniqueness, with each one viewing itself as the only possible channel for revealing God's desires and intentions for humanity. God, Ultimate Reality, or the gods are understood to be in charge of human life to some degree, but the different religious systems emphasize the extent of this control in different ways. Even with these different emphases, when humans have designed and practice religious traditions in hierarchies of direction and obedience, we position divinity or Ultimate Reality as an emperor of the cosmos. The imperial God becomes the only one who can determine every outcome, human or creaturely. Hierarchical religious traditions are a closed system that cannot actually experience life beyond its beliefs and practices as valuable, for the God who is at the top of their hierarchy is the only true God. All destiny, including the destiny of those humans and creatures outside the community, is in the hands of that only true God.

Claiming to hold the only valid experience of and relationship with God, hierarchical religious traditions depend on relatively recent notions of civilization to further their control in the world. Although that same ruling and revealing God created the universe many eons ago, hierarchical religious traditions claim that humans can only comprehend who God is and how God works in and through the patriarchal civilized epoch of recent millennia. In the last few centuries, as modern colonialism and industrial globalization have increased, these claims have taken advantage of human tendencies to project onto God several features that belong to ourselves and may have nothing at all to do with God.

Religion as Projection

Projection is a well-known psychological process. Positively, projection can evoke sympathy toward and understanding of others because we can comprehend what is going on in their life in the light of our own life experience. Negatively, projection has been described as a defense mechanism in which we seek to resolve our own uncomfortable feelings or perceptions by blaming others for them. It can also be employed to resolve situations of disempowerment by displacing onto others the features, or outcomes, we desire for ourselves. The "others" in question here may be other humans. They may be superhuman beings, deemed to be endowed with superb abilities.

In animist religious traditions, projection does not seem to have been a tool to separate us from our planetary life. We seem to have experienced sacredness within the fabric of creation itself. Both the joys and storms of the natural world were considered to be manifestations of the divine. In religious traditions that have held social power in recent millennia, projection can be a powerful basis for ignoring the relationships that we humans have with all other earthlings, prioritizing a super-human deity instead. This shift was probably influenced by and contributed to the emerging patriarchal consciousness as it was and is heavily preoccupied with domination and control. The patriarchal forces themselves felt the need for a heavenly validation, and imaging that the divine was a ruling patriarchal figure from above the sky gave that validation.

Instead of a new moment of divine revelation, this God-from-above-the-sky is an invented divinity, a projection of a patriarchal group's incessant need for validation and affirmation for its modes of governance. This divinity and this projecting act condemn humans to passivity, feelings of unworthiness, and senses of guilt and shame. Under this God, subservient humans are much easier for the patriarchs to control. Projecting our own desires for dominance, we end up imposing a judgmental God upon humans and the land alike.

Personalizing this all-powerful, dominating deity was a profoundly important theological development. The personalism that is employed, however, is itself highly problematic, for it reflects Classical Greek anthropology and adopts the rational and robust male individual as its ideal person. Declared to be the master of all that exists, this person named God has been encumbered with a multi-layered set of projections. Furthermore, each projected attribute is set in opposition to our flawed humanity and the broader flawed creation.

Naming the Projections

Raw hunger for power and domination has infiltrated so much of what we mean and understand by the notion of God. In

Christian theologies that same hunger has damaged, adulterated, and perverted our understanding of human personhood. We seek to redeem and restore the human condition by realigning it with our distorted notions of the divine.

Various denominations of Christianity have been heavily influenced by Classical Greek philosophy, supporting an image of God as a ruling patriarchal male. This anthropocentric depiction carries several projections related to the human craving for power and domination. Misinterpretation of Genesis 1:26–28 has contributed to humans further internalizing senses of supremacy over all other life-forms as a mandate from a supreme divinity. Uniquely fashioned in the image of God, humans mistake our creatureliness with a right to rule over everything as God does. We feel a need for an all-powerful personal deity, and this projection has generated a culture of co-dependency that empowers neither God nor humanity. These projections lead to several false and misleading characterizations of God and of ourselves.

A theological understanding of God as both all-powerful and personal may seem initially humane, friendly, and readily accessible through human encounters. Emphasis on the personhood of God has been expressed through various popular devotions and feasts in Christian history, and comfort and consolation are often the desired outcomes of these practices. Salvation is interpreted as life with the personal God. As the ultimate goal of human life, this salvation relationship largely misses any sense of an adult relationship with an adult God, collaborating to make life on earth more meaningful for all. Instead, God is believed to use divine omnipotence to deliver humans out of their suffering in this world.

As theologians and people attuned to the spiritual depth of life, we must re-vision the personal within the context of the transpersonal. In doing so, we may more accurately discern the theological mindset of our prehistoric ancestors and restore our relationships as earthlings to health. When humans remain very close to nature, as we seem to have done for much of our evolutionary story, we tend to honor transpersonal integration rather than protect the individual and isolated personal at all costs. How, then, do we reclaim a transpersonal understanding of God? How do we rework the tradition within a transpersonal context?

With Jeremy Lent (2017) we can view the entire creation in terms of patterning instincts. Everything, including humans, is interrelated and dynamic. This is an understanding that has been long endorsed by quantum science. From a Christian perspective, terms like *interrelated* and *dynamic* should immediately evoke the notion of God as Trinity.

Trinitarian theology has heavily relied on Classical Greek metaphysics since its emergence in the early church and its promulgation as doctrine since the Council of Constantinople in 381 AD. Such a reliance has focused on the one amid the many, the individual amid the collective. The "patterning instinct" gets lost in this focus and remains obscured for much of Christian theology today. Instead, I argue that we should view this doctrine as an archetypal statement for dynamic relationship. Whatever God means, Trinity denotes a deep capacity for relating before all else. We can best encounter, experience, and understand how God works throughout the entire creation when we recognize the dynamic relationships of Trinity. The Trinitarian understanding of God prioritizes the transpersonal over the personal.

Relational Aspirations

Nancy Abrams helps us to translate this patterning instinct into more human terms in her perceptive claim that our employment of the God-concept represents the sum total of human aspirations, particularly the desire to relate and connect at more subliminal or mystical levels. "God is endlessly emerging from the staggering complexity of all humanity's aspirations across time. . . . The idea that God is a phenomenon that emerges from human aspirations turns out to be astonishingly fertile" (Abrams 2015, 50). Her argument is both subtle and profound. The human relationship with God cannot be accurately described as a pact between an isolated powerful rule giver and an equally isolated obedient rule "getter." We are not isolated persons who either lord over or are subservient to others. Instead, we live through staggeringly complex relationships across time, and God intimately and dynamically emerges from each new moment. In Abrams's framing, the notion of God as simply a human projection or set of human projections is not bound to Classical Greek anthropologies. God projects through human aspirations, emerging from within humans' deep relational pursuits as earthlings. We cannot honor the full meaning of our humanity without engaging with such aspirational wisdom.

Our humanity emerges through our belonging to the cosmos through our belonging to the earth. We have inherited and are sustained by the evolutionary vitality of larger life systems that weave through one another. As Brian Swimme has noted, "In a most primordial way, we are cosmological beings" (Swimme 2022, 24). Our aspirations, desires, and longings, at conscious and subconscious levels, always belong to the transpersonal realm because they orient us to our own interconnectedness with other creatures. In the transpersonal, the human and the divine are intimately entangled.

Such entanglement is more readily comprehensible in Ilia Delio's recent work. Addressing the God-question in an evolutionary context, and echoing many insights borrowed from process theology, she writes:

> God simply cannot be considered apart from matter because, without matter, God-talk is impossible. God and world form a relational whole. . . . God is simply the absolute and ultimate whole who is becoming more and more whole in and through the entangled emergence of evolving life. . . . God and world co-create the universe as a whole because they are becoming something more together in evolution. It is not just creatures who are becoming new in evolution; God also is becoming new. . . . Evolution is the actualized personalization of divine love. (Delio 2023, 76, 82, 123, 246)

In the very becoming of creation at large, God also becomes. The mystery we call God becomes more transparent and available in the vast unfolding of evolutionary life, and the power of love that connects us more intimately with creation is how the transpersonal becomes more personalized.[2] Similar sentiments are echoed in the work of postmodern theologian John D. Caputo: "I do not take the name of God to be the name of a being, of an existent, but of a way I have been overtaken by the world" (Caputo 2015, 179). As we become more acquainted with the sacredness of creation itself, we are drawn into an experience of "divinity" not merely as a deeper dimension of our humanity but as an "insistence" that is integral to creation at large. Caputo explains it as follows:

> God insists, while we exist. . . . God is a spirit who calls, a spirit that can happen anywhere and haunts everything insistently. . . . The name of God is the name of an insistent call or solicitation that is visited upon the world, and whether God comes to exist depends on whether we resist or assist this insistence. . . . God is an insistence whose existence can only be found in matter, space, and time. Where else could God be God? (Caputo 2013, 13–14, 163)

We have inhabited matter, space, and time for millennia and are the inheritors of an evolutionary story that is millions of years in the making. Our desire to personalize God ironically risks depersonalizing God, abstracting God into philosophical categories—omnipotence, omniscience, immutability, impassibility—and puzzles—theodicy, heavy rocks, and square circles. We are in danger of forgetting that God is a life force that animates and sustains all the creatures with whom we share the web of life! Should our *animism*

---

[2] Ilia Delio's understanding of love, and particularly our love for God (best seen as our response to God's love for us), is heavily influenced by the work of Teilhard de Chardin.

be understood as an experience of divine insistence without feeling an urge to reduce it to a personal experience that is exclusively beneficial to each of us as individual human persons? Through classical Christian theology, what are the risks that accompany our objectification of God as an anthropomorphized entity who fits neatly into an Aristotelian construct of a robust individual?

For Christians, theological questions around the meaning of God often involve Jesus, his personhood, and his divinity. If we re-vision the Trinity through the transpersonal lens, Christian theologians have exciting opportunities to critically reengage Christology. Richard Rohr can helpfully focus our discussion on a possible christological next step. He distinguishes between Jesus as a historical person, who lived in Roman-occupied Nazareth some two thousand years ago, and Jesus as *the Christ*, who represents a sacred relational universality that transcends formal religion. Jesus as the Christ is a transpersonal force rather than a personal being:

> When the Western church separated from the East in the Great Schism of 1054, we gradually lost this profound understanding of how God has been liberating and loving all that is. Instead, we gradually limited the divine presence to the single body of Jesus, when perhaps it is as ubiquitous as light itself—and uncircumscribable by human boundaries. . . . Instead of saying that God came into the world through Jesus, maybe it would be better to say that Jesus came out of an already Christ-soaked world. The second incarnation flowed out of the first, out of God's loving union with physical creation. (Rohr 2019, 4, 15)

Our ancient ancestors, deeply immersed in the natural world, were experiencing a "Christ-soaked" creation long before they could name what was going on. It was an experiential realization of a sacred presence, real and tangible, without a need to individualize and personalize the experience. As we did emerge through evolutionary moments when we felt a need to personalize this divine insistence, we did not choose a God made in our own image. We recognized a transpersonal life force and called it the Great Spirit!

6

The Spirit Breaks Through

The natural world stands mute until it is spiritually encountered as saturated with grace and meaning.
—Mark Wallace

The Creator Spirit as ground, sustaining power, and goal of the evolving world, acts by empowering the process from within. God makes the world, in other words, by empowering the world to make itself.
—Elizabeth Johnson

Anthropological research on *animism* is better understood in terms of faith in the Great Spirit. Long before Plato and Aristotle proposed their various notions of soul, our ancient ancestors evidenced deep senses of the sacred. Our ancestors' sacred attentions seem to have involved a great deal more than the mere process of ensoulment. We are more than material stuff that is only made holy when infused with a soul.

It is unlikely that our hunter-gatherer ancestors, and their ancestors before them, thought of or perceived their world in the binary fashion of Classical Greek anthropology. Wholeness seems to have been a much more common experiential value. Material reality and spiritual reality were experienced as an intertwining whole. From its foundational immersion in the earth, Spirit inhabits everything. The diversity of the world manifests Spirit differently in various aspects of creation, but something of a Oneness underpins all (Harmless 2007; McGinn 2006).

In recent decades there has been a growing recognition of the importance of incorporating Indigenous perspectives and knowledge systems into so-called Western scientific practice, particularly in fields such as ecology and environmental management. Indigenous science refers to the knowledge systems and practices of Indigenous Peoples that are deeply rooted in their cultural traditions, sometimes called traditional environmental knowledge. Robin Wall Kimmerer notes that, "like scientific information, traditional knowledge arises from careful systematic observation of nature, from the results of innumerable lived experiments. Traditional knowledge is rooted in intimacy with a local landscape where the land itself is the teacher" (Kimmerer 2003, 101).

Even as the importance of Indigenous knowledge and wisdom is becoming more recognized, interpreting and applying their insights in contemporary contexts remains debated in settler-colonial societies. Indigenous Peoples themselves have been targeted for extermination in the name of modern progress. Their experiences of the world and the knowledge and wisdom that they have passed down through the ages have been interpreted as incompatible with values of economic and social progress. These racist mischaracterizations have prioritized particular kinds of human societies—European in origin, capitalist in economy, and industrial in scale—against the deeply observant, highly relational, and locally focused Indigenous societies across the world.

Exploring the Great Spirit

The value of the Great Spirit is one of many Indigenous insights that can challenge the social, anthropological, and ecological degradations of our time. Monolithic framing of Indigenous spirituality is unhelpfully reductive, for several contemporary cultures recognize the meaningful presence of Spirit in and throughout the world in a beautiful myriad of diverse spiritualities and ceremonies. Within this limitation,

I recognize an ancient, profound, and dynamic value in the Indigenous notions of the Great Spirit. Consequently, I suggest that practices of this earth-centered spirituality can provide valuable insights into how our ancient ancestors evolved their sense of spirituality, probably further back in time than ancient hunter-gatherers, and how we might become more responsible earthlings today.

Thoughts about the Great Spirit, as I have written elsewhere, seem to find agreement on a few elements amid tremendous cultural diversity.[1] Contrary to religious traditions that inherited Greco-Roman metaphysics, belief in the Great Spirit is not about intellectual assent to a set of propositions about some transcendent deity. Rather, Indigenous traditions prioritize a sensuous, visceral, emotional sense of connection with a spiritual life force that is immanent through material creation itself. There is an intensely felt affiliation with a powerful presence that is benign and empowering and, at times, fierce and overwhelming. Human access to the Great Spirit happens primarily through the soil of the land, its cultivation, seasonal produce, and nourishment for all sentient beings.

In these religious traditions we encounter no allusions to a personal God or a personal relationship with the Great Spirit in the style of Christian theologies. Yet, the Great Spirit is not an impersonal force. When we engage the Great Spirit in the world, we are engaging the transpersonal, including the personal realm, while simultaneously transcending it. Through their several rituals Indigenous communities strive to live in deep attunement with the Great Spirit.[2] Religious traditions are passed on by means of oral narratives, pictographs, cer-

---

[1] I elaborate on this topic in *In the Beginning Was the Spirit* (O'Murchu 2012).

[2] Worth recalling here is St. Paul's understanding of prayer as outlined in Romans 8:26: "The Spirit helps us in our weakness; for we do not know how to pray as we ought, but that very Spirit intercedes with sighs too deep for words." In other words, prayer is a form of receptivity and openness to the Spirit, and not merely a set of words or actions. In more mystical terms, prayer is something that happens to us, rather than something we create or perform.

emonies, and written texts. Ethical consciousness seems to be judged by the quality and care of the earth, recognizing its role in fostering and enhancing human growth, largely as it is understood in communal and tribal contexts.

Indigenous religious traditions value Spirit as an energy-force imbued with deep transpersonal meaning. At one level it is transcendent, belonging to something other than our own power. At another level, it may be described as a deeply intimate and relational force, embracing all living beings. The experiential sense of what is involved is vividly expressed in Robin Wall Kimmerer's popular works *Gathering Moss* (2003) and *Braiding Sweetgrass* (2013). She also calls the work an intertwining of science, spirit, and story, claiming that science can be enriched by a closer alignment with ancient Indigenous wisdom. Jeremy Lent's notion of a patterning instinct offers a good starting point as we plumb the deeper meaning, exploring how religion and spirituality can be equally enriched (Lent 2017, 2021).[3]

Can Christianity Accommodate the Great Spirit?

Today, pneumatology, the theology of the Holy Spirit, is one of the most exciting dimensions of Christian theology. Yves Congar, during Vatican II, bemoaned the centuries-long neglect of the Holy Spirit in theological work and pleaded for its rehabilitation in Christian thought. For Congar, the Holy Spirit, above all else, is a Spirit of Wisdom, unique, yet manifold. Without the Spirit we cannot understand the inner life of the Trinity itself, nor can we discern what an authentic relationship between humans and the church would look like. Congar operated very much within the Catholic context and strongly desired and supported further ecumenical interface. The charismatic renewal movement proved to be an area where that ecumenical dimension flourished in the second half of the

---

[3] Other sources serving this alignment with both science and spirituality include Raymond Pierotti (2011) and Gloria Snively and Lorna Williams (2016).

twentieth century. This movement marked a breakthrough from the more austere forms of prayer and worship to ones characterized by song, dance, and exuberant joy.

Amplifying the theology of the Holy Spirit across multi-disciplinary lines brings pneumatology into closer alignment with the notion of the Great Spirit. This amplification opens the opportunity to ask if our ancient ancestors were already attuned to understandings of God as energizing Spirit long before Christian theologians began that same exploration. Wolfhart Pannenberg was an important theologian at this expansive horizon. Having acquainted himself with field theory in physics, he began by asking how we could consider the Holy Spirit to be something akin to a cosmic field force, which, like the fields of gravity and electro-magnetism, pervades the entire universe.[4] He describes the Holy Spirit as the marvelous depth of life out of which all life originates (Pannenberg 1976, 106ff.).

For Pannenberg, the Spirit is the environmental network or "field" in which and from which creatures originate and flourish. By virtue of the fact that they are alive, creatures participate in God through the Spirit. The Spirit is the "force" that lifts creatures above their environment and orients them toward the future. The Spirit is the most comprehensive and powerful field from which all creatures derive the purpose and function of their existence: affirm life consistently. Wherever there is passion for life, there the Spirit of God is operating; life over against death, liberation over against oppression, justice over against injustice, and so on. To live by the Spirit is to affirm life unambiguously. The Spirit can also use the dynamics of vulnerability—as in sickness, pain, and trauma—to awaken solidarity and hope in those life experiences that do not yield easily to comprehension and meaning, a perspective vividly illustrated in the seminal work of Shelly Rambo (2010).

The Spirit is not just another field-force. It might well be envisaged as the force that energizes and animates all the fields

---

[4] "The field concept could be used in theology to make the effective presence of God in every single phenomenon intelligible" (Pannenberg 1988, 12).

upon which creation thrives and functions. Since the 1980s, scientific advances can help theologians view the Holy Spirit as this underpinning field for the various relational matrices that are known to Western science, Indigenous wisdom, and several Asian traditions (see Green 2011; Smolin 1997). Although not stated in such explicit terms, current thinking in pneumatology and process theologies, including Joseph Bracken and Veli-Matti Karkkainen, embrace this same insight (Bracken 1991; Karkkainen 2002, 2009).

Wolfgang Vondey is among the leading theologians carrying forward Pannenberg's pregnant insights (Vondey 2009, 2010). He provides an informative analysis of the significance of Spirit-force in the thinking of both Isaac Newton and Albert Einstein. For Newton, God is eternal in relation to time but ubiquitous in relation to space. The everywhere-ness of God may be compared to a subtle spirit pervading the entire natural world. Newton uses the notion of the ether to describe the dense energy sustaining everything in creation, and that ether is the vehicle for the activity of the living Spirit (Dobbs 1991, 101–2). Newton considered God to be the ultimate cause of everything that exists. God the Creator seems to be the one who acts from a distance, something akin to a great engineer. The Spirit, on the other hand, is more immediate and intimate, a universally present vitality. Vondey synthesizes Newton's pneumatology into five key points. First, Spirit is a necessary component for a philosophy of nature. Second, Spirit is an intermediate agent of the transcendent God in creation. Third, Spirit is a universal principle present in all natural phenomena. Fourth, Spirit is an internal medium of infinite duration (time) and extension (space). Fifth, Spirit is a cohesive and conforming force in nature (Vondey 2010, 82).

Einstein's understanding of the spirit at work in nature is quite different, Vondey notes. Einstein's special theory of relativity stripped the ether of its fundamental mechanical quality, rendering it an unnecessary hypothesis. For Einstein, Spirit is the rationality at work in the cosmic order, endowing the laws of nature with meaning and order, and bestowing an overall sense of unity and coherence in the workings of nature. Vondey recognizes five elements of the Einsteinian position. First, Spirit is a necessary component in the scientific endeavor. Second, Spirit is the rational order of the universe. Third, Spirit is a universal principle present in all natural phenomena. Fourth, Spirit is the symmetry of the space-time continuum. Fifth, Spirit has no physical material reality (Vondey 2010, 83).

As a Christian theologian, Vondey is pleased to see both eminent scientists acknowledging and addressing the force of Spirit at work in nature and in creation. He bemoans the fact the neither Newton nor Einstein makes any link with the personal, embodied identity of the Spirit as upheld by conventional Christian faith. On Vondey's part, the desire to protect the more personal interpretation of the Holy Spirit may in fact be inhibiting access to the transpersonal understanding of the Holy Spirit that we have discussed.

Moving beyond the Ex Nihilo Creator

In classic Christian theology, creation is largely the prerogative of God the Father. Though the Spirit hovers over the waters of Genesis 1 and all things come into being through the Logos of John 1, the doctrine of creation has traditionally focused on absolute divine authority to create *ex nihilo*, out of nothing. This claim upholds and affirms God's supreme authority but tells us little or nothing about the growth or evolution of creation after the divine creative act.

Process theologian Catherine Keller has argued for an alternative theology of creation's origins: creation *ex profundis*, creation out of the deep (Keller 2003, 155ff.). As the phrase implies, this creation arises out of the boundless and expanding depths of the chaos-cosmos rather than being zapped into being from nothing. "The beginning" does not mark a single absolute origin but a "beginning-in-process" that is both "unoriginated and endless."[5]

---

[5] For Keller, this interpretation is based on a thorough attention to the role of the Spirit in the opening verses of Genesis. Thus, for Keller, the Genesis narrative of creation begins with the Spirit, not with God the Father.

Peter G. Hodgson, another American theologian, has also recognized the value of this approach:

> Spirit is an immaterial vitality that enlivens and shapes material creation. It is the *energeia* that infuses all that is. . . . It is the relationality that holds things together even as it keeps them distinct. It is a desire or eros at once intellectual and sensuous. . . . Spirit is nothing without relations; it is precisely relationality, the moving air that permeates and enlivens things, the open space across which the wind of Spirit blows. (Hodgson 1994, 280, 284)

Theologian Gordon D. Kaufman, too, calls our attention to a new vision of creation and creativity:

> Instead of continuing to image God as the Creator, a kind of person-like reality who has brought everything into being, I have for some years been developing and elaborating a conception of God as simply the creativity that has brought forth the world and all its contents. . . . God is an activity rather than a person. (Kaufman 2004, xi, 48)

Theological challenges to classic Christian theological visions of creation as the sole act of an omnipotent divine actor open opportunities for further questions that benefit from a revaluing of the Spirit throughout the world. When anthropologists describe ancient belief systems in terms of animism, are they detecting something far more profound and sacred than a mere sense of nature being infused by a Platonic or Aristotelian soul? How could an organic, convivial, sensuous relationship with a powerful and empowering life force change our notions of animism past and present? Theoretical biologist and complex-systems researcher Stuart A. Kauffman's insight that "we do not need that supernatural God" might not be a dangerous challenge. Recognizing how "the creativity in nature is God enough" and that "God is our name for the creativity in nature

. . . can help orient us in our lives. Using the word God to mean the creativity in nature can help bring us to the care and reverence that creativity deserves" (Kauffman 2008, 142, 284).

For both our analysis of ancient prehistoric spirituality on the one hand, and a more empowering Christian theology for the twenty-first century, on the other, we are on more fertile territory in exploring links with the Indigenous notion of the Great Spirit. This is much more a God who is immersed in the evolving, emergent nature of life, a God whose presence is *persuasive* and *empowering* rather than manipulative and controlling. It is a God whose very becoming is enfolded into the evolution of creation itself.

Process theologians have it right. For some in this theological tradition, God is not envisaged as a person but rather as a transpersonal life force who can never be reduced to the physical creation. God yet percolates and informs every aspect of the world's growth and development. Revelation is not, then, a foundational set of revealed rational truths. God and God's desires for the world, for each creature in its own becoming, are revealed afresh in each moment as creation lives, moves, and happens. Over massive timescales, our evolution as creatures can certainly flourish and can certainly experience tragedy. God feels it all, journeying with us as co-creator.

Instead of trying to discern how God works in the world apart from the world's own life, I suggest that we need to discern more deeply the dynamics at work in creation itself. This discernment is a vital starting point for our Indigenous siblings and, for long, it probably was a vital starting point for our Indigenous ancestors. As we come to terms with how the divine operates in creation, we will also discern spirited clues into the meaning of divinity itself and its impact on our daily lives.

Instead of so much philosophical speculation in our theological approach, let us now adopt a more discerning disposition whereby we speculate less about the nature of God and instead seek to be responsive to the revelation of the Holy Mystery that surrounds us in the landscape of creation's own sacredness.

Both the mystery of God and the mystery of the human will be enriched in this process. As Gloria L. Schaab writes:

> Within the vivified, dynamic, and emergent self-creativity of the cosmos, God is revealed as continuously creative and immanent source of cosmic creativity in, with, and under the self-creativity of the cosmos itself. Moreover, this cosmic self-creativity is not to be understood as a separate movement or energy apart from or alongside the creativity of God as immanent and continuous Creator but truly as God-self immanently present and active in and through the self-creativity of the cosmos. (Schaab 2007, 138)

The Spirit of Paradox

For Indigenous Peoples, the Great Spirit is fundamentally a benign force, full of promise and hope. For some, it can also be the energy source of destruction, pain, and fragility. In the midst of storms, tornados, and earthquakes, the Spirit can be fierce, frightening, and overwhelming. Cheap theodicies that cleave the world into dualistic opposition of pure good and pure evil make no sense in a complex, entangled world. Indigenous Peoples have recognized the value of both-and instead of either-or as they experience and reflect upon the world. This apparent contradiction is viewed well as a paradox with evidence across the entire spectrum of the created universe. Here, we are called to integrate many experiences and plumb depths that I suspect only mystics can really comprehend or appreciate. Beverely Lanzetta invites us into this integral immersion, writing:

> A spirituality of benevolence avows to the unwavering constancy of the Great Spirit as ever present, neither judging, rejecting, arbitrary, violent, capricious, indifferent, or unforgiving. We are made and composed of Divine Love; we know a loving God who does not withdraw. We know a suffering God who bears the arrogance and deafness

of our small selves. . . . We honor the female ground of divinity while working to actualize the holiness of the Divine Feminine in our world. . . . We discover that all violation of truth is an aberration of the Great Mystery within us. We thus become excavators of our own truth, digging through the rubble of our anguish, confusion, and missed opportunities for the keys to where and how the spirit has been repressed or denied. Our life—in all its wonder and pain—is our teacher. It is through the process of spiritual awareness, love, and humility that we discover holiness within. (Lanzetta 2018, 119–20)

Such "within-ness" is not merely a personal sacred depth. It is transpersonal, across the whole gamut of creation, from the quarks and leptons to the open-ended universe itself. The Spirit knows no boundaries, no limitations. Caputo's elegant description of the divine insistence that "can happen anywhere and haunts everything" again resonates:

God is a spirit who calls, a spirit that can happen anywhere and haunts everything insistently. As to the big picture, the large course the Spirit traverses, the large circle it always cuts, there is no maybe about it; it must be what it must be. . . . God is an insistence whose existence can only be found in matter, space, and time. Where else could God be God? . . . There is grace, grace happens, but it is the grace of the world. My entire idea is to reclaim religion as an event of this world, to reclaim religion for the world, and the world for religion. (Caputo 2013, 131, 163, 346–47).

The creative energy of the universe is the primary gift of the empowering Spirit. Evolution is the long sacred story of the Spirit's energizing the world, characterized by creativity and paradox alike. Creative grace is not about escape from this world to a utopian paradise hereafter. That is just one of our several cruel delusions. As co-workers for and with the Great Spirit, our spiritual integrity is deeply embedded in Earth's own life. There is no heavenly world beyond, nor is there anywhere else to which we can escape. We must come to terms with this sacred space or, from here on, we will condemn ourselves to mass alienation.

7

Artificial Intelligence and the Evolutionary Human

The universe looks more like a great thought than a great machine. Mind no longer appears to be an accidental intruder into the realm of matter.... We ought rather hail it as the creator and governor of the realm of matter.
—James Jeans

We must remember that another and a higher science is also advancing with a giant's stride. It is the science of calculation—which becomes continually more necessary at each step of our progress, and which must ultimately govern the whole of the applications of science to the arts of life.
—Charles Babbage

Humans are a creative species, and our creativity flourishes when we remain very close to our creaturely kindred throughout the world, honoring our primary identity as earthlings. Contrary to popular anthropological assumptions that humans—particularly ruggedly individual, male, and white humans—are the biological victors of nature's survival of the fittest, paleoanthropology continues to surface evidence for our foundational capacity for creativity as a relationally interdependent species. These discoveries challenge the optimistic narratives of civilization that have prioritized human autonomy and mastery of the land through social and governance structures of control. Simply put, we must acknowledge the high price we paid for such "progress."

The structures of power and domination, particularly patriarchal domination, aimed to set us apart from all else in creation as the superior creature. We uprooted ourselves from more convivial, integrated ways of being that we had known for thousands of years. Though we brought with us deep wisdom from the past, we failed to integrate our underlying creativity and failed to remain close with the earth. Doing so would have been more consistent with our evolutionary development as earthlings.

As we move deeper in the twenty-first century, we seem to have arrived at another critical evolutionary threshold. Some theorists even claim that we have contributed to a new geological era, named the Anthropocene by some and characterized by human domination and control of the earth, paving the way for what seems to be a dangerously precarious future. In our precarity, technology is a horizon that both lures and launches us into realms of novel possibilities. Once more, our creativity is going to be crucial for human well-being. Perhaps, our ability to honor our identity as earthlings will be even more necessary than ever before.

Two features of that precarious future evoke special consideration at this time, namely the rapid rise of artificial intelligence (AI) and climate change. After briefly reviewing both, I propose that climate change might well be the catalyst for a more discerning analysis of AI and its prospects for our future evolution as a human species. In both cases, creativity will be of central importance.

The Rise of AI

The phrase *artificial intelligence* was originally coined in a 1955 paper by John McCarthy, Marvin Minsky, Nathaniel Rochester, and Claude E. Shannon. In this proposal for a conference at Dartmouth, they described the science and engineering of making intelligent machines. Matteo Pasquinelli has demonstrated how this work emerged through historical precedents going back to the mid-1800s. The 1940s and 1950s were a particularly fertile period that laid the foundations for current work in fields of AI research. In the latter half of the twentieth century this research cycled through advances, disappointments, and loss of funding. Notably, AI research has gathered more consistent momentum in the twenty-first century. Attention has shifted from possibility of creation to the existential risks that might be involved and what a relevant set of ethical guidelines might look like for these new technologies.

At one level AI is easy to grasp and understand. Following what we understand about the deductive processes of the human brain, we have trained machines to compute similar algorithmic tasks to those that our brains are capable of performing. In several cases we have discovered that machines can do such tasks much more quickly and efficiently than human beings. The ideal characteristic of artificial intelligence is its ability to rationalize and take actions that have the best chance of achieving a specific goal.

Machine learning (ML) is a subset of artificial intelligence research. ML refers to the concept that computer programs can automatically learn from and adapt to new data without being assisted by humans. Often ML is the category of AI research that raises fears and concerns about machines eventually taking over human life, rendering us irrelevant and even redundant.

Much of this research is based on a major underlying assumption that the human brain is essentially a machine. As a machine, what happens in the brain can be copied and transferred to other machines, particularly computers. Although this understanding of the human brain has been widely adopted across several branches of science, it is a partial view of the human brain that no longer enjoys extensive scientific support.

There are many practical uses of AI, and it is extensively used in our everyday lives whether we know it or not. Its range of applications include social media, digital assistants, maps and navigation resources, banking, facial recognition, medical robotics, and self-driving cars. Mustafa Suleyman, founder of DeepMind and Inflection AI, provides a range of other examples that touch virtually every sphere of human life, coming our way with a mixture of excitement and apprehension: "The [machines] will be the ones doing our work for us, finding information, assembling presentations, writing that program, ordering our shopping, advising on the best way to approach a problem, or maybe just chatting and playing" (Suleyman 2023, 284).

Incorporating machines into our lives may be more familiar than we realize. The pacemaker, for example, is a small, battery-powered device that is placed under the skin, near the collarbone, and prevents the heart from beating too slowly. First used in the early 1980s, it raised moral unease for some Christians. First, there was a fear that using the device was playing God as it could extend one's lifespan by several years beyond what God had intended. Second, living an extended life with the aid of a mechanical device was perceived as changing one's essential nature as a human being, resulting in becoming a cyborg rather than a divinely desired natural person. Largely, these concerns have fallen away and have done so rapidly. Virtually nobody today worries about the ethical implications of accepting and using such medical implants. To the contrary, many people would deem it to be morally irresponsible not to adopt such resources for a better quality of life.

The pacemaker is a very focused, implanted machine. It has a task, and the simplicity of this task is one of the reasons that theological and ethical reflection has been able to more readily deliberate on the moral good of adopting the pacemaker. When the machines become more complex, the theological and ethical considerations, likewise, become more complex.

One of the next stages in this development, the oft-referenced singularity, offers an important opportunity for our further consideration (Kurzweil 2005). Particularly as technology is being developed in the Western world, the time will come when a range of machines can be implanted in the brain by a local doctor, potentially changing human behaviors and regulating our bodily processes as we may wish or desire. Most people dread such a prospect, but one wonders if, in the years ahead, we will consider such a development to be another breakthrough with benefits that far outweigh its dangers.

Current human behavior on a global scale exhibits some deeply disturbing and destructive tendencies, seriously undermining the foundational creativity highlighted in this book. Suppose we develop brain implants that could modify and alter such behavior. How might such developments be advantageous to humans? Which humans might benefit more or less than others? Why? How might such developments be advantageous to other life-forms? How could these machines interface with the creativity that we have valued in this book? How will we bring our ancient creativity to bear upon the technology itself for ourselves and for the benefit of other life-forms? What priorities should guide the choices that we must make as individuals and as societies when we engage these technologies?

These questions are examples of a constellation of questions at the heart of how we as a species will deal with AI now and in the future. Suleyman has called some of these ethical concerns the containment problem (Suleyman 2023). In other words, it is important to identify who will be holding the power to identify, monitor, safeguard, and implement appropriate moral guidelines for these technologies and our use of them. Thus far, the AI community posits itself primarily as the moral judge and guardian, an arrangement that lacks the engagement and participation of the wider human and earthly communities. It is, therefore, unlikely to be either adequate or appropriate as AI gains greater prevalence in society.

Brain, Mind, and Consciousness

To better understand how human creativity enters this evolving process, we need to clarify what we mean by three central concepts: brain, mind, consciousness.

Brain

The brain is the most complex part of the human body. This organ is the seat of intelligence, interpreter of the senses, initiator of body movement, and controller of behavior. The brain receives and interprets all the sensory information, like sights, sounds, smells, and tastes. The human brain is a biological organ specialized for signal processing. It receives sensory input signals from all over the body and sends out motor signals to activate the muscles. Internal to the brain, signals are constantly circulating among 100 billion neurons. The rest of the nervous system is like a network that relays messages back and forth from the brain to different parts of the body.

From the perspective of AI researchers, the brain is a machine operated by biochemical properties, a view that has been adopted by many neuroscientists. This understanding arises from modernity's misperception of everything in creation, including the human being, as foundationally a machine that functions accordingly. However, the brain is a biological organ, not a digital computer. We must keep that in mind when discerning how AI influences our human lives and our world at large.

Mind

Many scientists perceive the brain and mind as complementary neural processes. The brain is never the same because it changes with every experience we have, every moment of every day. The mind is how we each uniquely experience life. It's responsible for how we think, feel, and choose. The physical brain responds to these unique experiences.

The mind can be understood as the driver of the human body, and the brain interacts with signals or instructions given by the mind. Brain and mind are both interrelated, interdependently entangled for the benefit of the person. Attempts to separate the two, to disentangle them, have plagued philosophers for centuries. Truly, they need each other to function properly.

Consciousness

The scientific study of consciousness was all the rage in the late 1800s, largely inspired by William James's *The Principles of Psychology* (1890). Additionally, Jungian psychology delves deeply into the meaning of consciousness and makes the notion more accessible to the general public. In the latter part of the twentieth century, with the advent of advanced brain scanning technologies, consciousness studies became more acceptable in rational scientific discourse.

Many cursory searches about and studies of consciousness highlight Daniel Dennett's work in his 1991 landmark book *Consciousness Explained*. For Dennett, consciousness is essentially a mechanistic process happening within the human brain, neurons interacting in response to various behavioral stimulations. It is a human phenomenon related to thought and perception, governed by material brain activity.

Other interpretations are emerging. Long associated with basic awareness, and related psychological states of perception, feeling, intuition, and imagination, consciousness studies are now stretching beyond the personal and interpersonal contexts, right into the very essence of creation itself. This new enlarged horizon is known as panpsychism. For the panpsychist, consciousness is inherent to even the tiniest pieces of matter, suggesting that the fundamental building blocks of reality have conscious experience.

In 1931, the renowned physicist Max Planck observed that consciousness is the fundamental stuff of all creation and that matter is derived therefrom. In this context, consciousness denotes information as a driving energetic force (Currivan 2017, 2–20). It is not merely an endowment of human intelligence. Consciousness is an empowering quality of creation in all its aspects and at every stage of its long historical evolution.

This enlarged horizon has a particular appeal to scientists influenced by quantum physics. Paul Levy, in *The Quantum Revelation*, writes:

> Being fundamental, consciousness can't be reduced to other features of the universe such as energy or matter. Thinking that the source of consciousness is in the brain is like looking in the radio for the announcer. . . . The brain does not produce consciousness; it is an instrument that tunes into and transmits it. Rather than generating consciousness, the brain may simply be a transducer that

acts as a filter as it mediates consciousness at the physical level. (Levy 2018, 279)

Contemporary American Teilhardian scholar Ilia Delio further recognizes that "consciousness is not a human phenomenon; nor does it pertain to the human brain alone. . . . We have come to understand consciousness as a cosmic phenomenon. Consciousness is integral to all aspects of cosmic life" (Delio 2015, 56, 58). In his detailed exploration of the patterning instinct across all aspects of universal life, Jeremy Lent has argued that "consciousness is not something that happens to us; it's an ongoing activity emerging through our engagement with the world" (Lent 2021, 184).

Consciousness and AI

According to physicist Jude Currivan, "Consciousness isn't something we have; it's what we and the whole world are" (Currivan 2017, 233). Consequently, we should ask how consciousness itself might influence and be influenced by the growing popularity of AI in our time. What possibilities could AI offer as an elevated threshold for self-reflexive consciousness? How could AI systems contribute to creation becoming more aware of itself in and through advances in human rational sciences and technology? In keeping with the broader focus of this book, how does AI interact with further evolutionary developments of our human capacity for creativity?

We also need to acknowledge a sociological dimension. Matteo Pasquinelli claims that the human adoption of technology long predated the neuroscience realm of AI and arose from the human engagement with labor and the various capacities for productive work.

> In short, the analytical intelligence of labor is what grounds the analytical intelligence of the machine. . . . In the twentieth century, it was information technologies that primarily reshaped society, as the mythologized vision of the "information society" implies; rather, it was

social relations that forged communication networks, information technologies, and cybernetic theories from within. Information algorithms were designed according to the logic of self-organization to better capture a social and economic field undergoing radical transformation. (Pasquinelli 2023, 68, 155; see also 134ff.).

While most of the leading advocates of AI are preoccupied with the neuroscience and its impact on human behavior and identity in our evolving future, my concern here belongs more to the realms of mind and consciousness. Here, we encounter aspects of our human lives and our broader world that seem to be beyond the remit of AI as currently defined. Since it seems that our self-consciousness and the consciousness of creation are inseparable, we are dealing with a phenomenon that cannot be reduced to or confined within what is essentially a mechanistic process.

Having received from creation the capacity to be aware, the quality and depth of our awareness contributes to and enriches the consciousness of creation. The mutual enrichment of that process very much depends on the quality of our attention and intention, two features that seem to be beyond the purview and control of AI. As computer scientist Melanie Mitchell notes, additional features of our human experience, such as imagination, intuition, desire, feeling, and our capacity for the aesthetic—so crucial to our human search for meaning—also supersede what intelligent machines can deliver (Mitchell 2019).

Much of the research into consciousness seeks to align it with the workings of the human brain, pursuing what specialists often call the hard problem of consciousness. If we recognize how consciousness belongs to a larger realm of our creative universe, as more quantum physicists seem to be suggesting, then we must face the possibility that the brain itself acquires its conscious capacity from the larger life systems. In this case we need to raise the question: From where does the universe obtain this wisdom? Scientists and theologians have hesitated to embrace an interdisciplinary resolution, but I find it important to journey on just such a path.

We must move to a higher level of discourse in pursuit of a deeper integration. In Christian theological terms, the Holy Spirit enlivens all that exists (Boff 2015; Haughey 2015). The pneumatology that I outlined in the previous chapter can expand our conversation by focusing on what some Indigenous Peoples around our world call the Great Spirit (O'Murchu 2012). Importantly, the experiential sense that the Great Spirit is not some transcendent deity above and outside the material creation but a life force made manifest to humans in and through a convivial relationship with the earth itself is a fertile sense for the discourse we need. The close affiliation with the natural world, which has been highlighted as a basis for our ancient capacity for creativity throughout this book, now takes on even a deeper meaning.

The Climate Emergency of the Twenty-First Century

While the research into AI raises a number of pressing issues for our time, they are not nearly as urgent as the climate crisis we are already experiencing. Through an increase of the concentration of carbon dioxide in the atmosphere, record-breaking weather changes—manifesting as hurricanes, floods, droughts, heat waves, wild fires, water shortages, and mass migration—are changing the very climate features of our planet. Fossil-fuel emissions seem to be the main culprit for the increase in carbon dioxide. Reduce the fossil fuels or, better still, get rid of them completely, and we can return the atmosphere to a more balanced equilibrium.

How can this solution work? Without fossil fuels we cannot create four essential commodities to the benefit of daily life: cement, steel, plastic, and ammonia that is needed to produce nitrogen fertilizer. The problem has reached critical levels as we have used more fossil fuels in the past thirty years than we did in all of previously recorded history. Green energy is vaunted as the hope for a better future, but metals are required to create computers, solar panels, electric vehicles, and all sorts of renewable technologies. Most electric vehicles are up to 50 percent plastic. Currently, electric cars run on lithium batteries, the production and disposal of which are extremely damaging to the environment.

The current climate crisis belongs to a much bigger evolutionary emergency, and our reactionary political and economic structures are addressing this emergency in a piecemeal and superficial manner. This approach makes the problem more intractable. We need more comprehensive strategies and practices.

When it comes to the evolution of life on the earth, and even the unfolding of the earth itself, climate change is one of the most enduring formative forces. Without shifting weather patterns—toward extremes of both hot and cold—we would not be inhabiting the world we know today. Destructive weather patterns are an integral feature of the great paradox of creation-through-destruction that has been described in Chapter 5. These historical changes do not, though, mean that we are absolved of culpability or responsibility. Instead, we must recognize how our deep creativity can shape our response to the current crisis.

For much of our seven-million-year evolutionary story, we and the predecessors to our species seem to have handled the dynamics of creation through destruction with remarkable wisdom and resilience. As I indicate in a previous work (O'Murchu 2012), faith in the Great Spirit seems to have been a central resource in recognizing the energizing ability that includes both the capacity to reinforce growth and wreak destruction. Being closely affiliated with the natural world, we learned to befriend the chaos of paradox rather than trying to conquer or eliminate it.

The current climate crisis, though, is a primary manifestation of our humanly driven ecological overshoot (Catton 1980). We have been using up the earth's ecological resources faster than they can regenerate, and we have been doing it for centuries. We have been forcing the finite resources of our world to feed our socioeconomic ideologies of unlimited growth and an insatiable desire to dominate and control. Our response, however it draws on our evolutionary story, must confront this new challenge as a new and unique crisis.

As we learn from our evolutionary story, we must learn to recognize how our desires for control and manipulation are connected to an ever-increasing disconnection from the body—our human bodies, the earth body, and the embodied dynamism of creation at large. The recent upsurge in AI is further evidence of the head running ahead of and away from the body. A more hopeful resolution for both the existential risks of AI and our climate emergency can come when we re-vision and reclaim our identity as earthlings.

Grounding Our Identity as Earthlings

We need to come down from the lofty heights of cerebral exploitation and reground ourselves once more in the home-context of our earth. We need to transcend our exceptionalism as a superior species and reclaim our more authentic identity as earthlings. In Christian terms, we need to reexamine the anthropocentrism that has interpreted our creatureliness made in the image and likeness of God as a justification for power-as-domination. We must redefine our place in the scheme of things as creatures born out of God's creation, unique like every other earth creature and superior to none. By reclaiming our earth-centeredness, we can then begin to address the anomalies and disconnections that undermine all sense of realistic hope for a better future.

In the fall of 1995 I participated in a workshop for a group of missionaries in Taiwan. The one-day event commenced with an individual exercise that required each of us to fill in a questionnaire called a "bioregional quiz." It consisted of twenty questions around issues like the sources of our daily food; the grasses, plants, and animals inhabiting a particular locality; recycling of waste products; and local methods of agriculture.

In terms of my childhood home in rural Ireland, I could answer seventeen of the twenty questions. In terms of my London location, where I had been living for over five years, I could only answer four of the twenty questions. The point of the exercise was to establish how well we knew our local bioregions. At the time I was not even sure what the concept of bioregionalism meant. The exercise clearly indicated that I was poorly grounded in my bioregion in London, whereas, in my childhood home in rural Ireland, I was intimately interconnected with the surrounding environment.

In scientific terms, bioregionalism denotes an area constituting a natural ecological community with characteristic flora, fauna, and environmental conditions and bounded by natural rather than artificial borders. Geologian Thomas Berry further elaborates:

> A bioregion is an identifiable geographic area of interacting life-systems that is relatively self-sustaining in the ever renewing process of nature. The full diversity of life functions is carried out, not as individuals, or as a species, but as a community that includes the physical, as well as the organic components of a region. Such a bioregion is self-propagating, self-nourishing, self-educating, self-governing, self-healing, and a self-fulfilling community. Each of the component life-systems must integrate its own functioning within this community to survive in an effective manner. (Berry 1985, 166)

Acquaintance with one's bioregion is one of the most effective ways of engaging with our earthiness as *Homo sapiens*. Therein we know the interdependent immediacy whereby our human life, and that of our co-partners in the bioregion, are entangled. Moreover, this is the bio-friendly coexistence we have known for much of our time as a species of the earth. It is also foundational to the prevailing creativity that has sustained and supported us through many a major crisis. How might attention to our bioregional locality be a foundational resource to sustain us amid the challenges of AI and climate change?

Super-Intelligent Earthlings

Much of the rhetoric around the evolution of AI is heady, cerebral, and excessively anthropocentric. Humans are vaunted as creatures endowed with an intelligence that supersedes all other life on earth, yet we feel threatened and insecure in the face of the posited super-intelligence of machines. In these frames the earth itself is once more perceived to be a commodity for human bartering, mastery, and control.

Much of this enterprise is driven by a range of irrational fears around control and domination. What we humans cannot master, we believe we can invent intelligent machines that will do it for us. In that process we think we can elevate our own potential to a point where all else on the earth is largely irrelevant and unnecessary. Even if we wreak havoc with our ecological overshoot, we assume that intelligent machines will rescue us from ultimate perdition.

AI certainly has benefits, but among its strong advocates there is a fantasized utopian anthropocentrism that, in the long term, is likely to further alienate the human from the creative web of life rather than integrate us in more coherent and life-giving ways. The rise of AI is an evolutionary imperative the benefits of which will only become apparent in some distant future. While we reap the benefits and wrestle with the dangers of AI, we must renew our commitment to our grounding in the earth, making the several adjustments that are now urgently needed if we are to become a more sustainable species to the benefit of all earth life.

The intelligence that will enhance a more empowering future for humans and all other life-forms belongs primarily to the creation itself in its cosmic and planetary giftedness. It is not the property of some super-intelligent machines modeled on narrow interpretations of the human brain. The consciousness that begets, sustains, and enriches life at every level transcends all our mechanistic achievements, arising instead from the spiritualized evolutionary momentum of creation itself.

Throughout our long evolutionary development, we have survived several critical evolutionary thresholds. Although we still lack precise evidence for how we achieved such breakthroughs, our creativity and intelligence were vital in seeing our ancestors through. That long-empowering narrative carries a will-to-meaning that will always outwit even the most intelligent machines we humans can invent. Perhaps the future will hold a collaborative endeavor among humans and intelligent machines that reinforces once more that ancient cooperative strain (Fuentes 2017, 7–10, 215–16). Mustafa Suleyman offers a provocative challenge: "Replicate the very things that make us unique as a species, our intelligence" (Suleyman 2023, 8). Our intelligence is not merely mechanistic computational efficiency. It is the relational resource that has seen us through many an evolutionary hurdle. Our future engagement with intelligent machines will not be one of marginalization or diminishment if we embrace our fullest intelligences.

8

Doing Theology in an Evolutionary Way

The presence of the wide evolving cosmos calls for a genuinely new paradigm, different from the anthropocentric concern with human sin in the context of feudal obligations. We need to turn the page on the satisfaction theory and allow it to take a well deserved rest.
—Elizabeth Johnson

Every being cries out silently to be read differently.
—Simone Weil

In 1989, Hans Küng and David Tracy published a book entitled *Paradigm Change in Theology*. The book emerged from a symposium held at the University of Tübingen and included contributions from, among others, Jürgen Moltmann, Edward Schillebeeckx, Leonardo Boff, Langdon Gilkey, and John B. Cobb Jr. The conference noted new horizons for theological engagement such as science, politics, feminism, and multi-faith dialogue. These topics did more than invite theologians into a wider discourse. They called forth new meanings of what theology signifies.

More recently, American theologian Matthew J. Frizzell has claimed that contemporary theology continues to be a site of extensive and growing religious dialogue that is concerned with the human predicament in late modernity and the nature of our ultimate concerns in light of diverse human perspectives, experiences, and cultures (Babie and Sarre 2022, 323–43). In the Catholic context, Pope Francis's ground-breaking encyclical *Laudato Si'* invited us to similar interdisciplinary approaches. Pope Francis called on Catholics and all people of good will to outgrow the world-hating and world-denying spirituality of the past and embrace the world as the site in which God engages us in our living faith in a more deeply integrated way. Whitney Bauman (2014) has further argued that crossing disciplinary boundaries is not entirely new for theology and religious traditions, noting how religion and science, humanity and nature, sacred and secular are always already intertwined. Attempts to separate them have been the result of particular metaphysical commitments, resulting in many of the destructive dualistic divisions that characterize our world today, especially in Western religious traditions.

As we have already noted, the omission of paleoanthropology from the interdisciplinary attentions of Christian theologians in recent decades is particularly striking. Theological anthropology has focused on far-more-recent history, offering a vision of the human person that has acted, and problematically at that, for only a few thousand years. The evolutionary story of *Homo sapiens* includes ancestry through myriad other species back nearly seven million years. It is far more interesting to engage the creativity of God at work in our species, our ancestors, and our world on this grander timescale. When we limit our theological anthropology to a narrowly reduced recent history, we cannot realistically expect anything other than a distorted vision of our humanity to be the result.

Tradition and Recapitulation

In Western Christian theological engagement with our humanity—theological anthropology—we tend to draw on a tradition that focuses on our flawed human condition. Tradition, while rooted in scripture, is influenced by each culture that inherits and interprets its practices, teachings, and values. As generations and cultures pass on, the tradition to subsequent generations, the teaching authority of the church and the local devotions and cultural philosophies of the faithful interact to shape the broader theological claims and teaching.

Contemporary theologians and scripture scholars frequently allude to reworking the tradition. Often, they do not go deep enough to recapture foundational truth. Western science advocates a strategy known as recapitulation, the biogenetic law that highlights how species often pass through the developmental stages of adult members of their species while in the embryonic stage. Recapitulation may also be described as the long-jump syndrome. We step back several stages from the jump-off point in order to gather momentum to leap forward several steps. Metaphorically, we are drawing energy from the deep past in order to engage more creatively with the emerging future.

The deep past that is typically invoked in Western Christian anthropology depends on a fall from grace as recorded in the story of Adam and Eve in the second creation narrative of Genesis. Some scholars have interpreted the social context of the story as a human struggle with the fertility of the land in the aftermath of the Agricultural Revolution (Taylor 2005; Snodgrass 2011). In this interpretation, humans were becoming ever more violent in their compulsive desire to dominate and control, and these violent projections influenced their understanding of a ruling God.

While the first chapter of Genesis describes the elegance and beauty of creation in the context of divine creativity, the remaining forty-nine chapters are largely about the human craving for power and the violent strategies adopted to achieve it. Commentators are quick to conclude that wayward humans disturb and destroy a divinely instituted equilibrium. As Karen Armstrong perceptively points out, reality is far more complex. God is creating the violent mess every bit as much as humanity:

> The God who dominates the first chapter of the Bible has disappeared from the human scene by the end of Genesis. Story after story reveals a much more disturbing God: as we shall see the omnipotent God of the first chapter soon loses control of his creation; the immutable deity

is seen to change his mind and even to feel threatened by humanity. The benevolent Creator becomes a fearful Destroyer. The impartial God who saw all his creatures as "good" now has favorites and teaches his proteges to behave in an equally unfair manner to their dependents. By the time we have reached the end of the text, almost every one of the expectations we were encouraged to form in Chapter 1 have been knocked down. (Armstrong 1996, 13)

With attention to the agricultural context, the symbolism of the Adam and Eve narrative can be read for insights into how humans may have related to the earth and its creativity prior to the rise of agriculture. Beyond the immediate literary or linguistic contexts, the garden can be interpreted as an archetypal abode of harmony and fruitfulness. The woman seems quite at home in the garden, enjoying an organic connection with the tree of life.

Eco-feminist interpretation highlights this connection and has further critiqued the historical interpretation of the woman and her organic link with the earth, the soil, and the land as evidence of misogynist bias in an emerging patriarchal society. Prioritizing masculine domination made space for—and at worst, actively promoted—the demonization of the female through her connectivity with the earth (Reid-Bowen 2007; Christ and Plaskow 2016). Taking the fruit from the tree of life is reinterpreted as an embodied expression of her own fertility, and the divine injunction against this action is framed as a patriarchal warning against the woman's natural flourishing. She wants to share the fruit with the rational patriarchal male, but he no longer knows how to receive it! Instead of viewing the avaricious male as the one who is out of step, the traditional interpretation blames the woman for the ensuing mess.

In a similar context, many commentators miss a deeper truth of the serpent. In ancient goddess cultures, the serpent was a symbol for creativity and the power of sexuality. It also denoted the process of transformation that leads to healing, hence the snake in the Caduceus symbol of medicine. The story in Genesis demonizes the symbol in the patriarchal drive to disempower—maybe, destroy—the power of the feminine principle. Little wonder that, from that moment on, violence erupts and becomes an integral dimension of the Genesis stories.

By attempting to honor a tradition of patriarchal interpretation, we short-circuit a broader and deeper tradition of human relationships with our planet as earthlings. We fail to go for depth, ending up with a perverse understanding of God and humans alike. From the intense research of our ancient human story, we can recognize that life was different from the long-assumed primitive barbarity. We seem to have prioritized relationship within the dynamic flows of the natural world, and the primacy of creativity in relationship can now reshape our interpretations of theological tradition. As we become ever more acquainted with that long, sacred story, claims of an original flaw that pervades our entire species becomes ever more incredulous and theologically unsustainable.

Confronting the Anthropocene

Theology for the twenty-first century must outgrow the dysfunctional Christian theological anthropologies of the past few thousand years. God's revelation in and through the human belongs to a much longer story. Increasingly, we are learning that ours is a story of mutual integration and not one of domination, manipulation, and compulsive control. From a divine perspective, the evolutionary mandate is one of creativity and cooperation rather than coercive lording over all other life, reducing the other than human to mere objects for marauding humans.

Consequently, the current label for the human enterprise—the Anthropocene—also needs a much deeper analysis. As early as 1873, Antonio Stoppani coined the term *anthropozoic* to describe the increasing negative impact of humanity on the earth's systems. In the early 1980s, Eugene Stoermer began using the term *anthropocene*, which, at the beginning of the present century, was popularized by atmospheric chemist and Nobel laureate Paul Crutzen. Within two decades, the word gathered momentum in elite scientific circles and appeared in nearly two hundred peer-reviewed articles.

The Anthropocene is envisaged as the sequel to the Holocene, marking the Holocene's demise amid the rapid rise of the Anthropocene. Typically, the evidence cited for this new evolutionary stage focuses on humans altering many features of the planet's ecological diversity, eventually leading to mass extinctions of plant and animal species, pollution of major waterways, including the oceans, and even altering atmospheric conditions. These multiple factors contribute to current crises such as global warming and destructive patterns of climate change. I wish to introduce and explore a metaphorical rather than geological meaning for the Anthropocene. Many of the ecological and environmental problems related to contemporary humans arise from an extensive and deep ignorance of the human species itself and our place within the earth. Currently, the Anthropocene largely bears negative connotations, describing the destructive impact of human behavior upon the earth's ecosystems, with climate change often cited as the primary example.

This rhetorical move risks scapegoating the human species writ large as a culprit to blame for the major ills of our time. While many of the major evolutionary shifts in world history are climate related, human contributions to the current crisis evidence how the changes that our world faces are the result of human behavior and the stories we tell ourselves about our place in the world as earthlings. We must, then, differentiate between the imperial Anthropocene and the evolutionary Anthropocene.

What I am calling the imperial Anthropocene describes the current perception that humans are driving many of the destructive forces at work in our world today. There is a great deal of truth in this assertion. Recognizing how these destructive behaviors are influenced and encouraged by imperialist anthropologies is, however, necessary. From an evolutionary perspective, calling this era merely the Anthropocene inaccurately equates human destruction with our entire species story and fails to recognize how particular social forces and structures have normalized power as dominance and control. What I am calling the evolutionary Anthropocene, instead, emphasizes how humans have been engaging our embeddedness in the earth for several thousands of years with a resilience and wisdom that has survived many major crises. It is important to recognize our culpability in the suffering of other humans, other than human creatures, and entire ecosystems of the earth. It is even more important to recognize how, as a species, we have faced major crises before and are now called to mobilize afresh our evolutionary resilience to confront the cultural deviancies that now absorb so much of our creativity. We must beget hew hope and possibility for a different and better future that is rooted in our seven-million-year evolutionary story.

Dutch social historian Rutger Bregman invites a similar reassessment:

> I'm no skeptic when it comes to climate change. There is no doubt in my mind that this is the greatest challenge of our time—and that time is running out. What I'm skeptical about, however, is the fatalistic rhetoric of collapse. Of the notion that we humans are inherently selfish, or worse, a plague upon the earth. I'm skeptical when this notion is peddled as 'realistic', and I'm skeptical when we're told that there is no way out. Too many environmental activists underestimate the resilience of humankind. (Bregman 2020, 136)

Why has our species become so problematic to our own well-being? What is our identity crisis? How do we negotiate its challenge? How do we see and understand our place in the world? What does our world mean for us, anyhow? "If we want to change the great challenges of our times from climate crisis to our growing distrust of one another," writes Bregman, "then I think the place we need to start is our view of human nature" (Bregman 2020, 9).

We do not need the wisdom merely to change the ways that we treat our planet and its resources. As Mustafa Suleyman notes:

Too many visions of the future start with what technology can or might do and work from there. That's completely the wrong foundation. Technologists should focus not just on the engineering minutiae but on helping to imagine and realize a richer, social, human future in the broadest sense. Technology is central to how the future will unfold—that's undoubtedly true—but technology is not the point of the future or what's really at stake. We are. (Suleyman 2023, 285)

We need a more drastic change. We need a whole new anthropology and a novel set of scientific and theological metaphors to tell the stories of ourselves. With new stories may even come new language to articulate the ancient depths of our evolving earthiness.

Creatures of a Relational Creation

Ours is a relational identity. However, our relationality does not begin with us humans. It is an endowment, an unsolicited gift with which we and all sentient beings are blessed. It is bestowed upon us by the universe itself.

Quantum physics posits this relational landscape as the ambience within which everything in creation grows and flourishes. The new cosmology redefines interconnectedness as the core stuff of the universe rather than the adversarial atomism that has driven modern sciences from anthropology and biology to physics. Throughout the closing decades of the twentieth century, theorists from a range of disciplines highlighted the central role of nature's inherent capacity for self-organization, scientifically named autopoiesis. Originally introduced by Chilean biologists Humberto Maturana and Francisco Varela in 1972, the concept highlights an internal symbiosis in living systems that cannot be explained in terms of cause-and-effect sequences. Though Maturana and Varela never linked the two, several commentators equate autopoiesis with the notion of self-organization (Jantsch 1980; Kaufman 2004).

Lynn Margulis highlighted the same relational orientation in the behavior of primordial bacteria, the organic basis of all life-forms. From the bacteria, to humanity, to the earth, and to the enveloping cosmos, relationality is the default position. Relationship is the vital link through which everything grows and flourishes. Even the destructive paradox inherently belongs to the relational web. Margulis vividly illustrates:

> Living beings defy neat definition. They fight, they feed, they dance, they mate, they die. At the base of the creativity of all large familiar forms of life, symbiosis generates novelty. It brings together different life-forms, always for a reason. Often, hunger unites the predator with the prey or the mouth with the photosynthetic bacterium or algal victim. Symbiogenesis brings together unlike individuals to make larger, more complex entities. Symbiosis is not a marginal or rare phenomenon. It is natural and common. We abide in a symbiotic world. (Margulis 1998, 9)

In the evolutionary Anthropocene, the challenge involves a great deal more than merely a more positive and creative view of the human condition. Nor is it merely about novel strategies in how we mutually and interpersonally relate. We are entering a radically expanded horizon of our anthropological identity. We can no longer live on our own, nor can we rely on a theology that keeps God at a static distance from the world. Neither this anthropology nor this theology makes sense in our evolutionary age. The critical issue now is our symbiosis with the natural world in all its paradoxical elegance, an endowment we have known down through the ages of our evolutionary story.

The human is central to what is unfolding in our time. Our superiority and domination pave a pathway of ruination for person and planet alike. We face an onerous and daunting choice between the imperial Anthropocene and the evolutionary Anthropocene. Both are possible. Only the latter is more congenial to our true life as earthlings.

If we prioritize the evolutionary Anthropocene, then we can embrace a very different human, planetary, and cosmic landscape. We can embrace a theological horizon that is appropriate for these new landscapes, one that is deeply relational and instinctively known for millions of years. Elizabeth Johnson offers a beautiful glimpse into this alternative anthropocentric horizon:

> A flourishing humanity on a thriving planet, rich in species in an evolving universe, all together filled with the glory of God: such is the vision that must guide us at this critical time of the earth's distress, to practical and critical effect. Ignoring this view keeps people of faith and their churches locked into irrelevance while a terrible drama of life and death is being played out in the real world. By contrast, living the ecological vocation in the power of the Spirit sets us off on a great adventure of mind and heart, expanding the repertoire of our love. (Johnson 2014, 286)

Johnson's relational vision embodies the ancient aspirations that have sustained us throughout several millennia of our evolutionary becoming. May the divine radiance throughout our evolutionary story empower us for the challenging times ahead—if we can risk all with courage and confidence.

Works Cited

Abram, David. 2010. *Becoming Animal: An Earthly Cosmology*. New York: Vintage Books.
Abrams, Nancy Ellen. 2015. *A God That Could Be Real*. Boston: Beacon Press.
Armstrong, Karen. 1996. *In the Beginning*. London: Vintage.
Babie, P., and R. Sarre, eds. 2022. *Religion Matters*. Singapore: Springer.
Bahn, Paul G. 1997. *Journey through the Ice Age*. Berkely: University of California Press.
Bar-Yosef, Ofer. 2002. "The Upper Palaeolithic Revolution." *Annual Review of Anthropology* 31: 363–93.
Bauman, Whitney. 2014. *Religion and Ecology: Developing a Planetary Ethic*. New York: Columbia University Press.
Berry, Thomas. 1985. *Technology and the Healing of the Earth*. Chambersburg, PA: Anima Books.
Bird-David, Nurit. 1999. "'Animism' Revisited: Personhood, Environment, and Relational Epistemology." *Current Anthropology* 40: S67-91.
Biviano, Erin Lothes. 2016. *Inspired Sustainability: Planting Seeds for Action*. Maryknoll, NY: Orbis Books.
Boehm, Christopher. 2001. *Hierarchy in the Forest: The Evolution of Egalitarian Behavior*. Cambridge, MA: Harvard University Press.
———. 2012. *Moral Origins*. New York: Basic Books.
Boeve, Lieven, et al. 2014. *Questioning the Human*. New York: Fordham University Press.
Boff, Leonardo. 1995. *Ecology and Liberation*. Maryknoll, NY: Orbis Books.
———. 2015. *Come, Holy Spirit: Inner Fire, Giver of Life and Comforter of the Poor*. Maryknoll, NY: Orbis Books.
Bowles, Samuel, and Herbert Gintis. 2013. *A Cooperative Species: Human Reciprocity and Its Evolution*. Princeton, NJ: Princeton University Press.

Bracken, Joseph. 1991. *Society and Spirit: A Trinitarian Cosmology.* Plainsboro Township, NJ: Associated University Press.

Bregman, Rutger. 2020. *Humankind: A Hopeful History.* New York: Bloomsbury.

Camp, Michael. 2023. *Breaking Bad Faith: Exposing Myth and Violence in Popular Theology to Recover the Path of Peace.* El Paso, TX: Quoir Publishing.

Cann, Rebecca L., Mark Stoneking, and Allan C. Wilson. 1987. "Mitochondrial DNA and Human Evolution." *Nature* 325: 31–36.

Cannato, Judy. 2006. *Radical Amazement.* Notre Dame, IN: Sorin Books.

———. 2010. *Field of Compassion: How the New Cosmology is Transforming Spiritual Life.* Notre Dame, IN: Sorin Books.

Caputo, John D. 2013. *The Insistence of God.* Bloomington: Indiana University Press.

———. 2015. *Hoping against Hope.* Minneapolis: Fortress Press.

Catton, William R. 1980. *Overshoot: The Ecological Basis of Revolutionary Change.* Champaign: The University of Illinois Press.

Challenger, Melanie. 2021. *How to Be Animal.* Edinburgh: Canongate Books.

Christ, Carol, and Judith Plaskow. 2016. *Goddesses and God in the World.* Minneapolis: Fortress Press.

Clegg, Brian. 2021. *Ten Patterns That Explain the Universe.* Cambridge, MA: MIT Press.

Clottes, Jean. 2008. *Cave Art.* London: Phaidon Press.

Clottes, Jean, and David Lewis-Williams. 1998. *The Shamans of Prehistory: Trance and Magic in the Painted Caves.* New York: Harry N. Abrams.

Collins, Christopher. 2013. *Paleopoetics: The Evolution of the Preliterate Imagination.* New York: Columbia University Press.

Cook, Jill. 2013. *Ice Age Art: Arrival of the Modern Mind.* The British Museum Press.

Crossan, John Dominic. 2010. *The Greatest Prayer: Rediscovering the Revolutionary Message of the Lord's Prayer.* New York: HarperCollins.

———. 2022. *Render unto Caesar: The Struggle over Christ and Culture in the New Testament.* New York: HarperCollins.

Currivan, June. 2017. *The Cosmic Hologram: In-formation at the Center of Creation.* Rochester, VT: Inner Traditions.

Dartnell, Lewis. 2019. *Origins: How the Earth Shaped Human History.* London: Vintage.

Darwin, Charles. 1859. *On the Origin of Species by Means of Natural Selection, or the Preservation of Favoured Races in the Struggle for Life.* London: John Murray.

Works Cited

Deacon, Terence. 1997. *The Symbolic Species: The Co-evolution of Language and the Brain*. New York: Penguin.

Deane-Drummond, Celia. 2014. *The Wisdom of the Liminal: Evolution and Other Animals in Human Becoming*. Grand Rapids, MI: Eerdmans.

Delagnes, Anne, and Helene Roche. 2005. "Late Pliocene Hominid Knapping Skills: The Case of Lokalalei 2C, West Turkana, Kenya." *Journal of Human Evolution* 48: 435–72.

Delio, Ilia. 2011. *The Emergent Christ: Exploring the Meaning of Catholic in an Evolutionary Universe*. Maryknoll, NY: Orbis Books.

———. 2015. *Making All Things New: Catholicity, Cosmology, Consciousness*. Maryknoll, NY: Orbis Books.

———. 2023. *The Not-Yet God: Carl Jung, Teilhard de Chardin, and the Relational Whole*. Maryknoll, NY: Orbis Books.

Dennett, Daniel. 1991. *Consciousness Explained*. Boston: Little, Brown, and Co.

De Waal, Frans. 2010. *The Age of Empathy: Nature's Lessons for a Kinder Society*. New York: Random House.

Dobbs, B. J. T. 1991. *The Janus Faces of Genius: The Role of Alchemy in Newton's Thought*. Cambridge: Cambridge University Press.

Farley, Wendy. 2011. *Gathering Those Driven Away: A Theology of Incarnation*. Louisville, KY: Westminster John Knox Press.

Fox, Matthew. 1983. *Blessed Unrest: The Way of Cosmic Renewal*. Santa Fe, NM: Bear & Co.

Frayer, David. 2016. "The Earliest Evidence for Right-handedness in the Fossil Record." *Journal of Human Evolution* 100: 65–72.

Fuentes, Augustin. 2017. *The Creative Spark: How Imagination Made Humans Exceptional*. New York: Dutton.

Gooley, Tristan. 2023. *How to Read a Tree: Studying the Patterns of Nature to Unlock Nature's Secrets*. London: Hodder and Stoughton.

Gowlett, J. A. J. 1984. *Ascent to Civilization: The Archaeology of Early Man*. New York: McGraw-Hill.

Graeber, David, and David Wengrow. 2021. *The Dawn of Everything: A New History of Humanity*. London: Allen Lane.

Green, Brian. 2011. *The Hidden Reality: Parallel Universes and the Deep Laws of the Cosmos*. London: Vintage.

Guthrie, Stewart. 2000. "A Comment." *Current Anthropology* 41, no. 1: 106–7.

Haight, Roger. 2019. *Faith and Evolution: A Grace-Based Epistemology*. Maryknoll, NY: Orbis Books.

Harmless, William. 2007. *Mystics*. Oxford: Oxford University Press.

Hart, Donna, and Robert Sussman. 2005. *Man the Hunted: Primates, Patriarchy, and the Origins of Human Violent Behavior.* New York: Basic Books.

Harvey, Graham. 2006. *Animism: Respecting the Living World.* New York: Columbia University Press.

Haughey, John C. 2015. *A Biography of the Spirit.* Maryknoll, NY: Orbis Books.

Haught, John F. 2010. *Making Sense of Evolution: Darwin, God, and the Drama of Life.* Louisville, KY: Westminster John Knox Press.

———. 2015. *Resting on the Future: Catholic Theology for an Unfinished Universe.* New York: Bloomsbury.

Heather, Peter. 2022. *Christendom.* London: Allen Lane.

Henshilwood, Christopher. 2009. "Engraved Ochres from the Middle Stone Age Levels at Blombos Cave, South Africa." *Journal of Human Evolution* 57: 27–47.

Hodgson, Peter C. 1994. *Winds of the Spirit: A Constructive Christian Theology.* London: SCM Press.

Horan, Daniel P. 2019. *Catholicity and Emerging Personhood: A Contemporary Theological Anthropology.* Maryknoll, NY: Orbis Books.

Howard-Brook, Wes. 2010. *"Come Out, My People!": God's Call out of Empire in the Bible and Beyond.* Maryknoll, NY: Orbis Books.

———. 2016. *Empire Baptized: How the Church Embraced What Jesus Rejected.* Maryknoll, NY: Orbis Books.

Hrdy, Sarah Blaffer. 2009. *Mothers and Others: The Evolutionary Origins of Mutual Understanding.* Cambridge, MA: Harvard University Press.

Jantsch, Erich. 1980. *The Self-Organizing Universe: Scientific and Human Implications of the Emerging Paradigm of Evolution.* New York: Pergamon Press.

Johnson, Elizabeth A. 1993. *Women, Earth, and Creator Spirit.* New York: Paulist Press.

———. 2014. *Ask the Beasts: Darwin and the God of Love.* London: Bloomsbury.

———. 2018. *Creation and the Cross: The Mercy of God for a Planet in Peril.* Maryknoll, NY: Orbis Books.

Karkkainen, Veli-Matti. 2002. *Pneumatology: The Holy Spirit in Ecumenical, International, and Contextual Perspective.* Grand Rapids, MI: Baker Academic.

———. 2009. *The Spirit in the World: Emerging Pentecostal Theologies in Global Contexts.* Grand Rapids, MI: Eerdmans.

Kaufman, Gordon D. 2004. *In the Beginning . . . Creativity.* Minneapolis: Fortress Press.

Works Cited

Kauffman, Stuart A. 2008. *Reinventing the Sacred: A New View of Science, Reason, and Religion*. New York: Basic Books.

Keller, Catherine. 2003. *Face of the Deep: A Theology of Becoming*. London: Routledge.

Kimmerer, Robin Wall. 2003. *Gathering Moss: A Natural and Cultural History of Mosses*. Corvallis: Oregon State University Press.

———. 2013. *Braiding Sweetgrass: Indigenous Wisdom, Scientific Knowledge and the Teachings of Plants*. Minneapolis: Milkweed Editions.

Kraybill, Donald B. 1990. *The Upside-Down Kingdom*. Scottdale, PA: Herald Press.

Küng, Hans, and David Tracy. 1989. *Paradigm Change in Theology: A Symposium for the Future*. Edinburgh, Scotland: T & T Clark.

Kuper, Adam. 2017. *The Reinvention of Primitive Society: Transformations of a Myth*. New York: Routledge.

Kurzweil, Ray. 2005. *The Singularity Is Near: When Humans Transcend Biology*. New York: Viking.

Langutt, Dafna, et al. 2021. "Climate and Environmental Reconstruction of the Epipaleolithic Mediterranean Levant." *Quaternary Science Reviews* 270: Article 107170.

Lanzetta, Beverly J. 2018. *The Monk Within: Embracing a Sacred Way of Life*. Sebastopol, CA: Blue Sapphire Books.

Lent, Jeremy. 2017. *The Patterning Instinct: A Cultural History of Humanity's Search for Meaning*. Amherst, NY: Prometheus Books.

———. 2021. *The Web of Meaning: Integrating Science and Traditional Wisdom to Find Our Place in the Universe*. Gabriola Island, BC: New Society Publishers.

Lévi-Strauss, Claude. 1966. *The Savage Mind*. Chicago: The University of Chicago Press.

———. 1978. *Myth and Meaning*. London: Routledge and Kegan Paul.

Levy, Paul. 2018. *The Quantum Revelation: A Radical Synthesis of Science and Spirituality*. New York: SelectBooks.

Lewis-Williams, David. 2002. *The Mind in the Cave: Consciousness and the Origins of Art*. London: Thames and Hudson.

Lieven, Dominic. 2022. *In the Shadow of the Gods: The Emperor in the World of Late Antiquity*. London: Viking.

Margulis, Lynn. 1998. *The Symbiotic Planet: A New Look at Evolution*. New York: Basic Books.

McGinn, Bernard. 2006. *The Essential Writings of Christian Mysticism*. New York: Modern Library.

McFague, Sallie. 2001. *Life Abundant: Rethinking Theology and Economy for a Planet in Peril*. Minneapolis: Fortress Press.

McIntosh, Christopher. 2004. *Gardens of the Gods: Myth, Magic, and Meaning*. London: I. B. Tauris.

McPherron, Shannon P., Zeresenay Alemseged, Curtis W. Marean, Jonathan G. Wynn, Denné Reed, Denis Geraads, René Bobe, and Hamdallah A. Béarat. 2010. "Evidence for Stone-Tool-Assisted Consumption of Animal Tissues Before 3.39 Million Years Ago at Dikika, Ethiopia," *Nature* 466: 857–60.

Meier, John P. 1994. *A Marginal Jew: Rethinking the Historical Jesus*, vol. 2. New Haven, CT: Yale University Press.

Mitchell, Melanie. 2019. *Artificial Intelligence: A Guide for Thinking Humans*. New York: Farrar, Straus and Giroux.

Moore, Lucy. 2022. *In Search of Us: Adventures in Anthropology*. London: Atlantic Books.

Oakley, Kenneth P. 1949. *Man the Tool-Maker*. London: British Museum (Natural History).

O'Murchu, Diarmuid. 2008. *Ancestral Grace: Meeting God in Our Human Story*. Maryknoll, NY: Orbis Books.

———. 2012. *In the Beginning Was the Spirit: Inquiry into the Emerging Life World of Ancestral Consciousness*. Maryknoll, NY: Orbis Books.

———. 2017. *Incarnation: A New Evolutionary Threshold*. Maryknoll, NY: Orbis Books.

———. 2018. *Beyond Original Sin: Recovering Humanity's Creative Urge*. Maryknoll, NY: Orbis Books.

———. 2021. *Doing Theology in an Evolutionary Way*. Maryknoll, NY: Orbis Books.

———. 2023. *Eco-Spirituality: Toward a Planetary Spirituality for Our Times*. Maryknoll, NY: Orbis Books.

Oppenheimer, Stephen. 2003. *The Real Eve: Modern Man's Journey out of Africa*. New York: Basic Books.

Pannenberg, Wolfhart. 1976. *Theology and the Philosophy of Science*. Philadelphia: Westminster Press.

Pasquinelli, Matteo. 2023. *The Eye of the Master: A Social History of Artificial Intelligence*. New York: Verso.

Pettitt, Paul. 2022. *Homo Sapiens Rediscovered: The Early Record of Human Modernity*. London: Thames and Hudson.

Pierotti, Raymond. 2011. *Indigenous Knowledge, Ecology, and Evolutionary Biology*. New York: Routledge.

Primack, Joel R., and Nancy Ellen Abrams. 2007. *The View from the Center of the Universe: Discovering Our Extraordinary Place in the Cosmos*. New York: Penguin Publishing Group.

Rambo, Shelly. 2010. *Spirit and Trauma: A Theology of Remaining*. Louisville, KY: Westminster John Knox Press.

Reid-Bowen, Paul. 2007. *Goddess as Nature: Towards a Philosophical Theology*. Burlington, VT: Ashgate.

Renfrew, Colin, et al. 2009. *The Sapient Mind: Archaeology Meets Neuroscience*. New York: Oxford University Press.

Renfrew, Colin, and Michael J. Boyd. 2016. *Death Rituals, Social Order, and the Archaeology of Immortality in the Ancient World*. New York: Cambridge University Press.

Ridley, Matt. 1998. *The Origins of Virtue: Human Instincts and the Evolution of Cooperation*. New York: Penguin Publishing Group.

Rifkin, Jeremy. 2010. *The Empathic Civilization: The Race to Global Consciousness in a World in Crisis*. Cambridge, UK: Polity.

Rohr, Richard. 2019. *The Universal Christ: How a Forgotten Reality Can Change Everything We See, Hope For, and Believe*. New York: Convergent Books.

Schaab, Gloria L. 2007. *The Creative Suffering of the Triune God: An Evolutionary Theology*. New York: Oxford University Press.

Schick, Kathy D., and Nicholas Toth. 1994. *Making Silent Stones Speak: Human Evolution and the Dawn of Technology*. New York: Simon and Schuster.

Simard, Suzanne. 2021. *Finding the Mother Tree: Discovering the Wisdom of the Forest*. New York: Knopf.

Smolin, Lee. 1997. *The Life of the Cosmos*. Oxford: Oxford University Press.

Snively, Gloria, and Lorna Williams, eds. 2016. *Knowing Home: Braiding Indigenous Science with Western Science, Book 1*. Victoria, BC: University of Victoria.

Snodgrass, John. 2011. *Genesis and the Rise of Civilization*. North Charleston, SC: CreateSpace.

Spong, John Shelby. 2016. *Biblical Literalism: A Gentile Heresy*. New York: HarperOne.

Stewart, John E. 2000. *Evolution's Arrow: The Direction of Evolution and the Future of Humanity*. Rivett, ACT: Chapman Press.

Stout, Dietrich. 2016. "Tales of a Stone Age Neuroscientist." *Scientific American* Special Edition 25, no. 3: 28–35.

Suleyman, Mustafa. 2023. *The Coming Wave: Technology, New Science, and the Innovation That Will Change Everything*. London: The Bodley Head.

Swimme, Brian Thomas. 2022. *Cosmogenesis: An Unveiling of the Expanding Universe*. Berkeley, CA: Counterpoint.

Swimme, Brian, and Evelyn Tucker. 2011. *Journey of the Universe*. New Haven, CT: Yale University Press.

Swimme, Brian, and Thomas Berry. 1992. *The Universe Story: From the Primordial Flaring Forth to the Ecozoic Era, A Celebration of the Unfolding of the Cosmos*. New York: HarperOne.

Tanner, Kathryn. 2005. *Economy of Grace*. Minneapolis: Fortress Press.

Taylor, Steve. 2005. *The Fall: The Evidence for a Golden Age, 6,000 Years of Insanity and the Dawning of a New Era*. Winchester, UK: O Books.

Torrey, E. Fuller. 2017. *Evolving Brains, Emerging Gods: Early Humans and the Origins of Religion*. New York: Columbia University Press.

Vearncombe, Erin, Michael Peppard, and Hal Taussig. 2022. *After Jesus Before Christianity: A Historical Exploration of the First Two Centuries of Jesus Movements*. New York: HarperOne.

Vondey, Wolfgang. 2009. "The Holy Spirit and the Physical Universe: The Theological Cosmology of Isaac Newton." *Theological Studies* 70, no. 3: 3–36.

———. 2010. *Beyond Pentecostalism: The Crisis of Global Christianity and the Renewal of the Theological Agenda*. Grand Rapids, MI: Eerdmans.

Woodburn, James. 1982. "Egalitarian Societies." *Man* 17, no. 3: 431–51.

Wohlleben, Peter. 2023. *The Heartbeat of Trees: Embracing Our Ancient Bond with Forests and Nature*. Vancouver: Greystone Books.

Worrall, Simon. 2017. "How Creativity Drives Human Evolution." *National Geographic*, April 23.

Yong, Ed. 2022. *An Immense World: How Animal Senses Reveal the Hidden Realms around Us*. London: The Bodley Head.

Index

Abram, David, 19, 30, 33, 36–37, 39, 119
Abrams, Nancy, 76–77
Acheulian archaeological sites, 56, 57, 58
Adam, 111, 112
After Jesus Before Christianity (Vearncombe et al.), 44
Age of Empathy (De Waal), 43
Agricultural Revolution, 5, 29. 49, 52, 63, 69
    Adam and Eve narrative and, 111
    denigration of pre-Agricultural Revolution, 33
    Genesis narrative in the lens of, 19–20
    hunter-gatherer culture prior to, 54–55
    rise of the Agricultural Revolution, 6
    shadow side of the Agricultural Revolution, 10
animism, 65, 74
    anthropological notions of, 71, 88
    divine insistence, as an experience of, 78–79
    Great Spirit and, 81
    sun worship, as associated with, 13
    Tylor, use of term by, 64, 67
anthropic principle, 38
Anthropocene
    confronting the Anthropocene, 113–16
    evolutionary Anthropocene, 117–18
    as a new geological era, 94
anthropology, 55, 111, 117
    bankrupt anthropology, 5–8
    contemporary anthropology, 9, 26, 28
    Greek anthropology, 7, 8–10, 11, 32, 53, 74, 77, 81
    inherited anthropology, 21, 22, 30, 35, 41
    new anthropology, need for, 116
    paleoanthropology, 2, 3, 4, 17, 23–27, 93, 110
    theological anthropology, 10, 110
Aquinas, Thomas, 9

Aristotle, 11
  Greek anthropology, as a key figure in, 7, 8–9
  humans, distinguishing from the rest of creation, 10
  soul, on the notion of, 31, 40, 64, 71, 81
Armstrong, Karen, 111–12
artificial intelligence (AI), 43, 59, 98
  AI research, 95, 98, 102
  consciousness and, 100–2
  evolution of, 94, 100, 105–6
  existential risks of, 104
  rise of artificial intelligence, 94–97
atonement theology, 70
Augustine of Hippo, 66
Australopithecus, 23, 27, 58
autopoiesis, 116

Babbage, Charles, 93
Babie, P., 110
Bauman, Whitney, 110
Berry, Thomas, 105
Bhimbetka petroglyphs, 61
biblical literalism, 16
bioregionalism, 41, 104–5
Bird-David, Nurit, 64
Biviano, Erin Lothes, 3
Boehm, Christopher, 42–43, 55
Boeve, Lieven, 9, 10
Boff, Leonardo, 3, 109
Bowles, Samuel, 43
Boyd, Michael J., 28
Bracken, Joseph, 86

Braiding Sweetgrass (Kimmerer), 84
brain, 59, 61, 101
  brain implants, dread over potential for, 96–97
  brain size in human ancestors, 27–28
  consciousness, brain as a transducer of, 99–100
  describing and defining, 97–98
  Homo habilis, brain of, 12, 56
  machines as modeled on, 95, 106
  toolmaking, brain activation during, 57
  wisdom, differentiating from brain development, 26
Bregman, Rutger, 115
Broom, Robert, 23
Brueil, Henri, 63
Brunet, Michel, 27

Caduceus symbol, 112
Camp, Michael, 7
Cann, Rebecca, 26
Cannato, Judy, 38
Caputo, John D., 78, 91
Catton, William R., 103
chaîne opératoire approach, 57
Christ, Carol, 112
Christian Councils, 9, 16, 66, 76
Christology, 79
climate change, 53, 94, 102–4, 105, 114, 115

Index

Clottes, Jean, 63–64
Collins, Christopher, 61
companionship of empowerment, 45–49, 50
Congar, Yves, 84
Congregation for the Doctrine of the Faith, 72
consciousness
  artificial intelligence and, 100–102
  brain, mind and, 97–98
  describing and defining, 98–99
  ethical consciousness, 84
  evolutionary momentum of, 106
  human consciousness, 17, 64
  imperial consciousness, 52, 62
  patriarchal consciousness, 74
Consciousness Explained (Dennet), 99
Constantine, Emperor, 1, 16, 44, 50
the containment problem, 97
cosmic identity, 11–12
cosmology, 17, 116
the cosmos, 73, 77
  creation *ex profundis* arising from, 87
  deeply held narratives on, 36
  the evolving cosmos, 66, 109
  relationality of the enveloping cosmos, 117
  self-creativity of the cosmos, 90
cosmotheology, 2
Council of Carthage, 66
Council of Constantinople, 9, 76
Council of Orange, 66
Council of Trent, 16
creation *ex profundis*, 87
Crossan, John Dominic, 45–46
Crutzen, Paul, 113
Currivan, Jude, 99, 100

Dart, Raymond, 23
Dartnell, Lewis, 38
Darwin, Charles, 1, 3–4, 69
Dawkins, Richard, 34
Deacon, Terence, 60–61
De Anima (Aristotle), 8
deep time, 13, 27–28, 50, 62
Delagnes, Anne, 56–57
Delio, Ilia, 3, 67, 77, 100
Dennett, Daniel, 99
Descent of Man (Darwin), 4
De Waal, Franz, 43
Dikika archaeological site, 58
Divine Feminine, 91
Dobbs, B. J. T., 86
dogmatism, 15–17
Dubois, Eugène, 23

ecology, 41, 69, 82, 118
  ecological community, 105
  ecological concerns, 3, 44
  ecological diversity, 114
  ecological niches, 68

ecological overshoot, 103, 106
ecological spirituality, 16
egalitarianism, 41, 42–43, 44, 55, 70
ego-explosion, 6, 21
Einstein, Albert, 86–87
Empathic Civilization (Rifkin), 43
empathy, 19, 43, 70
ethics, 39, 84, 95, 96, 97
eudaimonia (happiness), 8
Eve, 111, 112
evolution, 10, 11, 26, 56, 75, 77, 110
  biological evolutionary theory, 21
  consciousness, historical evolution of, 99
  contemporary evolutionary emergence, 44
  creation in the evolutionary story, 54, 87, 89
  creativity as part of human evolution, 24, 29
  cultural evolution, 2, 67
  Darwin on evolution, 4, 69
  of earthlings, 36–39, 54
  East Africa as the human origin point, 38, 50
  egalitarianism in early human evolution, 55
  empathy and entropy, co-evolution of, 43
  end of the evolutionary line, humans as, 71
  evolutionary Anthropocene, 113–15, 117–18
  evolutionary emergency of climate change, 103–4
  future evolutionary success, 42
  God in evolutionary life, 5, 50, 78, 80
  hominin evolution, 4, 17, 25, 29–31, 57
  original sin and, 29, 66
  post-Agricultural evolution, 32
  the sciences, as established in, 34–35
  as the Spirit energizing the world, 91
Ex Nihilo Creator, 87–90

faith, 110
  alternative visions of, 16, 118
  Christian faith, 44, 49–50, 87
  cultural philosophies of the faithful, 111
  evolutionary story and, 5, 36
  gospel-based faith, 45
  Great Spirit, faith in, 81, 103
  human narrative as a faith story, 28–32
  multi-faith settings, 72–73, 109
fallen humanity, 20, 21, 34, 52, 66, 70, 111
Farley, Wendy, 46
Florisbad Skull, 25
fossils, 4, 102
  Ethiopia, fossil finds in, 25, 27
  Homo fossils, 23–25, 56, 58

at Jebel Irhoud, Morocco, 25–26
Leakeys, search for, 22–23
Fox, Matthew, 29, 66
Francis, Pope, 29, 41, 110
Frayer, David, 56
Frizzell, Matthew J., 109–10
Fuentes, Agustin, 55, 59–60, 107

Gathering Moss (Kimmerer), 84
Genesis
  on the Garden of Eden, 66
  Genesis narrative, 111–12
  misinterpretation of, 75
  stories of creation in, 19–20, 52, 53, 87
Gintis, Herbert, 43
goddess cultures, 112
Gowlett, J. A. J., 58
grace
  as abounding, 65–66
  creative grace, 91–92
  fall from original grace, 34, 52, 111
  natural world as saturated with, 81
Graeber, David, 13, 51, 53, 54, 55
Great Schism, 79
Great Spirit, 50, 80, 102
  animism of ancient times and, 64–65
  Christianity theology and, 84–87, 89
  exploring the Great Spirit, 82–84
  faith in the Great Spirit, 81

  as the Spirit of Paradox, 90–92
Green, Brian, 86
green energy, 102
Guthrie, Stewart, 64

Haight, Roger, 48
Haile-Selassie, Yohannes, 27
Harmless, William, 82
Hart, Donna, 30
Harvey, Graham, 64
Haughey, John C., 102
Haught, John F., 2–3
Heather, Peter, 44
Henshilwood, Christopher, 60
Hierarchy in the Forest (Boehm), 42–43
hierophany, 68
Hinduism, 40, 52
Hodgson, Peter G., 88
Holocene era, 114
Holy Spirit, 17, 65, 84–85, 86, 87, 102
Homo erectus, 12, 24–25, 26, 58
Homo ergaster, 25, 26
Homo habilis, 12, 23–25, 26, 28, 56
Homo neanderthalensis, 13, 28, 61, 64
Homo sapiens, 59, 105
  Darwin on, 3–4
  evolutionary story of, 25–26, 29–30, 110
  Homo habilis, brain similarities with, 28, 56
Horan, Daniel, 32

Howard-Brook, Wes, 31, 48–49
Hrdy, Sarah Blaffer, 43

Ice Age, 13, 55, 59, 63, 64
imago Dei, 8, 32
Indigenous Peoples, 86, 89
    Great Spirit, understanding of, 90, 102
    Indigenous spirituality, 64–65, 82–84

James, William, 98
Jantsch, Erich, 116
Jeans, James, 93
Jebel Irhoud, 25–26
Jesus Christ, 22, 30, 40, 44
    companionship of empowerment and, 45–46
    evolution and the coming of historical Jesus, 50
    Genesis story, framing within Jesus narrative, 66
    reign of God, proclaiming, 48–49
    resurrection as releasing grace of, 65
    Rohr on Jesus as the Christ, 79
Johanson, Donald, 27
Johnson, Elizabeth, 48, 81, 109, 118

Kant, Immanuel, 19
Karkkainen, Veli-Matti, 86
Kauffman, Stuart A., 88
Kaufman, Gordon D., 88, 116
Keller, Catherine, 1, 16, 87
Kimeu, Kamoya, 25
Kimmerer, Robin Wall, 82, 84
kingdom/reign of God, 45, 46–49, 50
Kirchhoffer, David G., 9–10
Kraybill, Donald B., 47
Küng, Hans, 109
Kurzweil, Ray, 96

language, evolution of, 12, 61
Lanzetta, Beverly J., 90–91
Laudato Si' encyclical, 29, 41, 110
Leakey, Louis and Mary, 22–23
Leakey, Richard, 25
Ledi-Geraru research area, 58
Lent, Jeremy, 12, 61–62, 76, 84, 100
Leroi-Gorham, Andre, 63
Lévi-Strauss, Claude, 63, 68
Levy, Paul, 99–100
Lévy-Bruhl, Lucien, 68
liberation theology, 3
Lieven, Dominic, 52
Lokalalei archaeological site, 57
Lomekwi archaeological site, 58
Lovejoy, Owen, 27
Lucy, discovering fossil finds of, 27

machine learning (ML), 95
Man the Tool-maker (Oakley), 24

Index

Margulis, Lynn, 117
Maturana, Humberto, 116
McCarthy, John, 94–95
McFague, Sallie, 3
McGinn, Bernard, 82
McPherron, Shannon, 58
the mind, 98
Minsky, Marvin, 94–95
Mitchell, Melanie, 101
Mitochondrial Eve, 26
Moral Origins (Boehm), 43
Moss, Candida, 49–50
mystical spirituality, 16, 76, 90–91

National Geographic (periodical), 23
natural selection, 69
Nature (journal), 26
neuroscience, 58–59, 98, 100–101
Newton, Isaac, 86, 87
New Zealand, 65
Ngeneo, Bernard, 25
Nichomachean Ethics (Aristotle), 8

Oakley, Kenneth, 24, 60
Oldowan archaeological site, 24, 56–57
Olduvai Gorge, 23–24, 56
On the Origin of Species (Darwin), 3
Oppenheimer, Stephen, 26
original blessing, 29, 66
Origins of Virtue (Ridley), 43
Out of Africa hypothesis, 26

Paleolithic era, 42, 43, 61, 63
Pannenberg, Wolfhart, 85, 86
panpsychism, 99
Paradigm Change in Theology (Küng/Tracy), 109
Pasquinelli, Matteo, 95, 100–101
patriarchy, 6, 7, 30, 32, 112
　patriarchal church history, 45
　patriarchal consciousness, 74
　patriarchal context, 52–54
　patriarchal culture, 10, 72
　patriarchal domination, 94
　patriarchal God, 1, 43, 73, 74, 75
　patriarchal religion, 21, 41, 113
Peppard, Michael, 44, 49–50
personhood, 8, 65
　God, personhood of, 75
　individuality, relationship, and personhood, 13–15
　individualized understanding of, 9, 10
　inherited sense of personhood, 31
　Jesus, personhood of, 79
　paleoanthropological understanding of, 17
Planck, Max, 99
Plaskow, Judith, 112
Plato, 7–8, 31, 40, 64, 71, 81
pneumatology, 84–86, 102. *See also* Holy Spirit
postmodernism, 17, 78
primates, 11, 22, 43
Primitive Culture (Tylor), 67
Principles of Psychology (James), 98

process theology, 77, 86, 89
progress, myth of, 54
projection, 31, 111
  God as a human projection, 4–5, 30, 74, 75, 77
  naming the projections, 74–76
  religion as projection, 73–74
Protestant Reformation, 16

Quantum Revelation (Levy), 99

Rambo, Shelly, 85
Reid-Bowen, Paul, 112
religion, 16, 67, 91
  in evolutionary trajectory, 40, 62–65
  formal religion, 13, 33–35, 39, 49, 62, 79
  human evolution and, 5, 22, 61
  Jesus of Nazareth on, 48–49
  management and control, using for, 72–73
  negative view of life in, 51–52
  patriarchal religions, 21
  as projection, 73–74
  science and, 2, 3, 110
Renfrew, Colin, 24, 26, 28, 59
restrictive language hypothesis, 60
Ridley, Matt, 43
Rifkin, Jeremy, 43, 69–70
righteousness, 47, 49
Roche, Helen, 56–57
Rochester, Nathaniel, 94–95
Rohr, Richard, 79

Sahelanthropus tchadensis, 12, 27, 50
salvation, 2, 20–22, 62, 75
the sapient mind, 59
Sarre, R., 110
Savage Mind (Lévi Strauss), 68
Schaab, Gloria L., 90
Schick, Kathy, 55–56
Scholastic philosophy, 9
Schwager, Raymund, 7
Science (journal), 24
serpent symbology, 112
shamanism, 63–64
Shannon, Claude E., 94–95
silvology, 15
Simard, Suzanne, 15
sinfulness
  anthropocentric concern with, 109
  Christian myth of sin and redemption, 22
  original sin, 21, 28, 34
    Christian notions of, 33, 39
    in the evolutionary story, 30
    original blessing *vs.*, 29, 66
  Paul on the sinfulness of the human condition, 65
Smolin, Lee, 67
Snodgrass, John, 111
sociopolitical evolution, 7, 52
Spong, John Shelby, 47, 70
Stewart, John E., 42

Stoermer, Eugene, 113
Stone Age Institute, 55–56
Stoppani, Antonio, 113
Stout, Dietrich, 24, 58–59, 61
Suleyman, Mustafa, 59, 107
  on future technology, 115–16
  on the practical uses of AI, 95–96
  on the promise and peril of AI, 43–44
survival of the fittest, 51, 93
Sussman, Robert, 30
Swimme, Brian, 11, 77
symbiosis, 116, 117

Tanner, Kathryn, 3
Taung Child, 23
Taussig, Hal, 44
Taylor, Steve, 6, 21, 111
technology, 55, 71, 94
  brain scanning technologies, 99
  ethical guidelines for, 95
  information technologies, 100–101
  Oldowan lithic technology, 24
  renewable technologies, 102
  stone technology, 28, 56, 58, 61
  technological entrepreneurs, 43–44, 116
  tool technology and brain size, 57
  trajectory of, 38, 59, 96–97
theology of human fulfillment, 70
therianthropes, 63–64
Torrey, E. Fuller, 13
Toth, Nicholas, 55–56
Toumaï skull, 27–28
Tracy, David, 109
traditional environmental knowledge, 82
transpersonalism, 14, 31, 75–80, 83–84, 87, 89, 91
trees, 12, 15, 24, 36, 64, 112
Trinity, 76, 79, 84
Turkana Boy, 24, 25
Tylor, Edward B., 64, 67

Varela, Francisco, 116
Vatican II, 84
Vearncombe, Erin, 16, 44, 49–50
Vondey, Wolfgang, 86–87

Wallace, Mark, 81
Weil, Simone, 109
Wengrow, David, 13, 51, 53, 54, 55
White, Tim D., 27
Whitehead, Alfred North, 33
Williams, David Lewis, 63, 64
Wong, Kate, 1
Woodburn, James, 54–55
Worrall, Simon, 60